ACTRESS

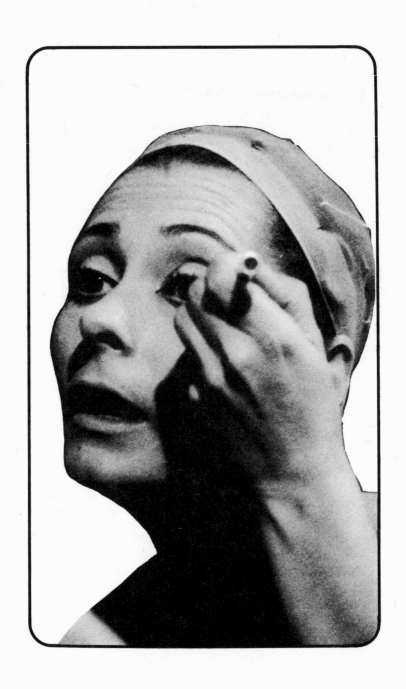

ACTRESS
POSTCARDS FROM THE ROAD

ELIZABETH ASHLEY
WITH ROSS FIRESTONE

M. EVANS & COMPANY, INC. NEW YORK

Library of Congress Cataloging in Publication Data

Ashley, Elizabeth, 1939-
   Actress: postcards from the road.

   1. Ashley, Elizabeth, 1939-   2. Actors—United
States—Biography.   I. Firestone, Ross, joint author.
II. Title.
PN2287.A77A32   792'.028'0924 [B]   78-17218
ISBN 0-87131-264-6

M. Evans and Company, Inc.
216 East 49 Street
New York, New York 10017

Design by Ginger Giles

Manufactured in the United States of America

9 8 7 6 5 4 3 2 1

This book is dedicated to everyone who ever bought a ticket to anything—everyone who ever wondered what it's like to be up there—out there—in there. This book is for the audience.

Key to Photographs

Opposite title page: making up for *Caesar and Cleopatra*

Page 5:   upper right, Beulah Beatnik; bottom, the dressing table

Page 11:   upper right, custom fitting for *Caesar and Cleopatra;* bottom, with McCarthy

Page 17:   upper right, with Garland, Redford and, Beatty (photo by Sam Siegel); middle, cover *Life,* November 22, 1963 (courtesy of *Life* magazine); lower right, at dressing table (photo by A. E. Woolley)

Page 32:   *Ship of Fools*

Page 57:   upper right, our wedding; center, *Carpetbaggers;* bottom, me n' George

Page 78:   top, limos, mink coats, and red carpets; bottom, autographs

Page 90:   top left, with Christian and George; top right, Christian, 1977; bottom, with Christian, 1970

Page 103:   top right, rehearsing for *Carpetbaggers* with Jose Greco; bottom left, London, 1964

Page 123:   top, Hollywood; middle left, publicity shot (photo by Ellen Graham); bottom right, back at work (photo by Penelope Breese)

Page 135:   top right, with Michael Kahn and Tennessee Williams; bottom left, Maggie; lower right, with McGuane (photos by Martha Swope)

Page 171:   top right, with McGuane (photo by Martha Swope); bottom left, *92° in the Shade.*

Page 196: top left, Beulah Beatnik; top right, lines (photo by A. E. Woolley); bottom right, Jimmy Farentino.

Page 216: top left, alone (photo by A. E. Woolley); top right, with Jimmy Farentino at our wedding party, 1962; bottom, with Art Carney in *Take Her, She's Mine* (photo by Fred Fehl)

Page 240: top left, first pose; bottom left, summer in the country; right, *Caesar and Cleopatra*

Introduction

Three times in my life publishers have come to me and given me money to write a book. Twice I took a shot at it, took a look at the shot, then gave the money back. I'm not a writer. Wish I were, but them's the breaks.

In 1975 I did a long taped interview for a book called *The Success Trip*. The interviewer was a fortyish hipster who didn't seem to have the slightest interest in the usual show business palaver. I told him more truth than I ever told any shrink. A year later we were approached about doing a book together. I hemmed and hawed, then said, "Why not?"

It seems to me that the American people have been processed to assume they are never told the whole truth about famous personalities and events. Most of the time this assumption is correct. They aren't.

Media hype dictates that there always has to be a separation between private reality and public image. The reasoning goes like this: The public cannot be trusted with the raw truth about the rich, powerful, famous and infamous because if the public *really* knew what *really* went on it would turn on the subjects of the hype like sharks in a feeding frenzy. P.R. people, like television Standards and Practices people, are forever telling senators and presidents, movie stars and athletes, joint chiefs of staff, bareback riders, singers and dancers just how limited, bigoted and intolerant the "people in the boonies" are.

6

Bullshit.

I am a moderately famous, slightly aging lady of stage, screen, and TV who has been privileged to spend the last twenty of my thirty-eight years traveling all over this country, getting up in front of thousands (maybe millions) of Americans, dancing my dance, singing my song, and saying my poem from motel to motel, bar to bar, laugh to laugh, paycheck to paycheck. I've gotten to hang out with cowboys and presidents, smugglers and cops, movie stars and teamsters, farmers and millionaires, intellectuals and illiterates, and I know one thing for sure: You can tell an American the truth about anything and if you are really straight you are probably in for a terrific conversation. You may not get agreement, but you will almost certainly have a good, hot, rich exchange. Curiosity, compassion, and imagination are the most consistent spiritual characteristics I have found in the American psyche.

This book is not an autobiography. It is about how I found my ticket to ride.

Elizabeth Ashley
Santa Monica, California

ACTRESS

Last night I came close to breaking. Fear, despair and exhaustion converged on me, and I had no resources left to fight back. I was dry. Wrung out. Mentally, physically, and emotionally wasted. Terror was winning, and in two hours I would have to go onstage and do a show that is in serious trouble.

It started when Dean, my dresser, came into the dressing room and asked where to set the prop for my new entrance in Act Two. I couldn't understand the question. I heard the sound but was unable to process the words. My brain had stopped functioning. I couldn't make language.

It took all the physical energy I had left not to break everything in the room. I wanted to throw the makeup off my dressing table. Smash the mirror. Hurl the cassette player against the wall.

I sat there holding onto the sides of the chair and heard myself scream. Then I began to cry.

McCarthy, my husband, was playing his guitar in the next room where Lynne was combing out my wigs. They rushed through the doorway, then froze when they saw what was happening to me. Somehow I managed to put the words together.

"EVERYBODY GET THE FUCK OUT OF HERE!"

I knew if they stayed I would do something horrible. I was breaking, and when you break you don't break alone. You smash up everyone around you, especially those you love best.

By seven-thirty, a half hour before curtain, I pulled myself together, went on and did the show. I can do that because that's the last thing that goes. And when you're out there, everything else stops. For awhile.

But I woke up this morning with a gut ache and chills. More than anything, I wanted to pull the covers over my head and hide. I couldn't. I was scheduled to work with the speech coach from ten until noon, rehearse from twelve to five, then do another performance at eight. We open in New York in three weeks and need every second left to get this production off the ground or at least moving down the runway. The out-of-town reviews were disastrous, and the play is being entirely restaged with a new director. We work on the new show during the day, then play the old show at night, adding whatever changes we can.

McCarthy got me out of the hotel and drove me to the theater. By the time I finished the two hours of vocal exercises I was hyperventilating badly. During rehearsal I became feverish, then dizzy and chilled. I felt as if I was going to vomit. I was gagging but hadn't eaten anything, so there was nothing to throw up. Later this afternoon the doctor came. He thought it might be a virus but didn't really know. There were about two hours left before curtain, so I lay down on my dressing room couch and napped for an hour. Then I had to get myself ready to go out there again.

McCarthy was sitting next to me as I put on my makeup. Dean and Lynne were laying out my costumes and wigs. There was a knock on the door, and a couple of stagehands and truckers ambled in and plopped themselves down.

"Hey, Bessie, we hear you're feelin' like shit. Here,

13

this is for you."

I looked at the small packet of tinfoil one of them held out to me and asked him what it was.

"It's some coke, man. Go on. Do it. It'll make you feel better."

Now everyone knows, even though they don't dare say so, that cocaine can get you up to do a show. It may not be the best thing for you, but it's far from the worst. And it works. Especially if you're sick and down.

I was handing them back their coke because I knew they couldn't afford to give it away when there was another knock and a third stagehand walked in. He smiled and held out two rolled joints.

"Here, man, this will straighten out your stomach."

All of us looked at each other and broke up.

Then Dean led me out to the backstage elevator. I rode up and did the performance, and it seemed to go all right. And as I sit here now in my hotel room at two in the morning I'm starting to feel better even with all the exhaustion and sickness, and I'm thinking maybe we'll get this show flying yet.

The point is not that they brought me cocaine and grass.

In another age it would have been a bottle of bourbon.

The point is that I am not some kind of "star" to them. They see stars come and go and they know that's not at all what I'm about. Stagehands are people who work just as hard as I do. They understand when you need a gift, when you need a stroke, when you need whatever it is you need. They are my friends. My dressing room is a place where they come to take a break, tell me what's going on, and share the way working people share whatever they have. It's a six-pack of beer more often than not. But I have learned as much about what I do for a living from electricians, grips, sparks, and flymen as I have from Lee Strasberg. Those people are the lifeblood of the theater, the tendons and sinews.

And I am part of what they are part of.

We are all carnival people.

We are all laborers.

I think that to do whatever you do with any vision you have to have a precise picture of your place on the cultural map. I don't want my place to be as a Lady of the Theater. That's a meaningless thing today. What I am is a laborer, a blue collar worker with aspirations toward art. Art is my vision, my dream, the fruit I would like my efforts to bear. But when you get right down to it, I am, like those stagehands, another laborer in the carnival.

The function of the carnival is to mirror the underbelly of the culture and the time. My job is not to tell you about the mores and manners of our society or the politics and commerce. That's the job of the novelist. What I'm supposed to be a specialist in is what people *don't* say, *don't* show, what never rears its head in polite society. People pay all that money to sit in a chair in the theater mainly because it is a respectable way to see and experience things they cannot see and experience in their own lives. And I believe that if we are going to serve our function and mirror that underbelly, then we have to traffic in it. I know in my soul that the most important thing for me is to remain always an outlaw—emotionally, mentally, spiritually, and legally—and to keep close touch with the traffic that exists beneath respectable, conventional society.

It's the one thing that makes what I do for a living

15

interesting because nine times out of ten the gigs themselves are not interesting.

My reward is in my existence.

Most performers don't feel that way, which is why
they lose their roots and are always at the mercy of their
jobs. I will spend my life searching for parts and plays
that have something to say and rarely ever finding them.
But as long as I can continue on with my existence, even
the pain, frustration, and failure are all somehow worth
it.

LIFE

ELIZABETH ASHLEY
BROADWAY'S
BRIGHTEST
AND NEWEST

NOVEMBER 22 · 1963 · 25¢

1

The same day President Kennedy was shot dead in Dallas, Texas, my picture was on the cover of *Life* magazine. The caption: "Elizabeth Ashley: Broadway's newest and brightest."

To the outside world I was the hottest young actress around. The year before I had won a Tony Award for *Take Her, She's Mine,* and now I was starring on Broadway with Robert Redford in *Barefoot in the Park.* Neil Simon had written the play for me, and it was the biggest hit in town. You couldn't even buy a ticket. I was also the big buzz in the movie of *The Carpetbaggers.* The critics hadn't liked it much, but they gave me terrific notices and the picture was raking in millions of dollars at the box office. I had it all, including a famous movie star in love with me. I was twenty-two years old and all my dreams had come true.

I ended the week locked away in the psychiatric ward of Payne Whitney Hospital.

Welcome to the Sixties, Bessie Mae.

It started while I was walking crosstown late in the afternoon on my way to the theater. I was going to work. As I waited for the light to change on Lexington Avenue, my sensory circuits blew and for a moment I went blind. Everything turned dark, the way it does if you stare directly into the sun. I could still hear the traffic, but I couldn't see it. Then I began to see the sounds. They looked like colored ribbons. A definite brain warp.

I stood there, unable to place one foot in front of the other. People bumped into me as they tried to get past. Finally, someone took me by the arm and led me across.

A voice asked, "Can I help you?"

I said, "I'm okay, I'm okay. Just please, can you get me into a cab?"

The driver dropped me off in front of the theater, and I made it to my dressing room, my oasis. I sat down at my makeup table and tried to get ready for the show. But I couldn't do that either. I kept staring at the makeup. I couldn't figure out what to do with it. Then I got the shakes and sobs.

Time was closing in. I knew I would not be able to go out there on the stage that night.

And I didn't want to go out there.

The show had become an agony of self-consciousness and despair for me. I was getting famous and hot and everyone was telling me how terrific I was. But I didn't feel terrific. I felt like a failure. I had a lot of energy and flash and was as adorable as I could be. But I wasn't any good and I knew it. I could tell that Redford knew it too, and every time I went out on the stage it compounded my sense of inadequacy.

I wanted so deeply to be good but didn't know how. The more I acted the worse I seemed to get. There was absolutely no sense of accomplishment. I felt I had gotten lucky and scored, and of course all that does is make you paranoid. You start to feel that everyone who looks at you sees that you're just a hustler who pulled a fast one and the next time you throw the dice they're going to come up low.

It was all in my own head space because it didn't

matter to anyone else whether or not I was good. That was never discussed. It was taken for granted that I was as good as I needed to be. I had, after all, scored and scored big. But I wanted to be a fine actress, an artist. That was the only noble thing I knew. And the more successful and famous I got, the more of a joke that became.

I didn't know how to deal with it. I was totally dependent upon the outside world for my existence. I am who they say I am. I am who they think I am. I am only as they see me. That's who I am. In a room by myself with the door closed there wasn't anybody there.

George Peppard was the one person who really understood the kind of pressure that was on me. But he wanted me to give it up. When I tried to talk to him about it, he would say, "Well, that's the way it goes. That's what an actress' life is like. Do you want your life to be like that? It's a fucked way to live. Don't do it. Marry me and you won't have to."

What he said made sense. But I wasn't ready to give it up. It was the only thing of my own that I had.

As I sat in my dressing room and felt the minutes passing, I became more and more afraid. I held on to the edge of the makeup table to try to feel something solid, and bit my mouth as hard as I could to keep it closed. I couldn't get a sentence or thought going, and I knew if I opened my mouth just once I would start to scream and babble. It was like trying to sit on a tidal wave.

Then the stage manager walked in. I tried to answer his question, and the scream began.

They got me out of the theater and into a cab and put the understudy on in my place. All the way down to my apartment I kept lacerating myself for missing the show. It wasn't the first one I'd blown. I had already been out much too much.

"Failure, failure, failure! You can't make it. You're

a cop-out. You're no good. You don't have what it takes. You never did. You never will."

My shrink was there waiting for me when I got home. I was barely coherent, and I shrieked at him over and over, "I confess, I confess! I can't do it! I give up, I give up, I give up!"

I suppose I was surrendering to my failure, to my inability to cope with anything, to do anything. I could not put one foot in front of the other. I could not get across the street. I could not go out on the stage. Everybody who had invested money and hope and trust in me was going to be let down. I couldn't take it. I'd lost. I'd failed at everything and now I had broken.

"You've got to help me," I sobbed. "I can't go to the theater any more. I can't do the play. I don't know what's the matter with me. If I don't get some help, I'm going to kill myself. I'm going to take the pills or something. I'm no good and I can't stand it that I'm no good. I can confess it and surrender to it, but I can't face it."

When I ended my tirade, he looked at me and said, "Okay." Then he took me off to Payne Whitney.

I was grateful.

They put me in a bed and shot me up with heavy drugs. Now I was a kid who had been loaded a lot and knew a thing or two about dope. What I didn't know was that what gets you high on the street is small change next to what the good doctors will pop you with.

I fell asleep, but the dreams came on just like they always did. Whatever devils and demons were inside me kept right on turning their tricks, Demerol or no Demerol.

It was the middle of the day in a crowded street in New York. I was naked and running around like some deranged animal, trying to find a way to cover myself.

21

People were staring at me, pointing and laughing. I cowered down behind a mailbox, but they followed me, and I kept scuttling around it to conceal my nakedness. A lady walked by in a coat. I grabbed at it, but the other people laughed and pulled it away. They started after me and I ran and ran and ran. . . .

I was by myself on the top of a skyscraper, grasping the iron railing with both hands. The wind was trying to blow me over. I did my best to hold on, but it was too strong. I went over the side and listened to myself scream all the way down.

I woke up in a cold sweat. At least I thought I woke up, but I couldn't be sure. The dream might have taken a new turn. Maybe I had flipped out completely.

Something was in the room with me, whimpering urgently just a few feet away. It sounded like a caged animal crying for its life. The room was dark, but from the light that came in through the open door I made out this quivering mass moving around down toward the foot of my bed. It was jiggling, trembling, dancing while it mewled and cried like some sort of mad, wounded creature.

I screamed.

A woman rushed in and grabbed the thing. She yelled at it—"Dammit! You're not supposed to be in here!"—then dragged it out through the doorway.

I lay there holding on to the sides of the bed and tried to get my brain to process where I was and what had happened. I was still stoned from all the drugs they had shot into me, and it took a while to figure out I was in the hospital. That's right; I was supposed to be in a play, but I couldn't go on because the doctor had put me here.

I waited for whatever was going to happen to happen. When nothing did, I made an effort to get up but was pulled back down by the strap that had been buckled around my waist. The sleeve of my right arm was also pinned down with a large safety pin. A rubber tube led out of my arm to a bottle of something hanging next to the bed.

I called out, "Anybody! Anybody!" until the nurse came back into the room.

"Jesus, what's going on?" I asked her.

"Don't worry. Everything's all right."

She was a little too placating.

"Was somebody in here?"

"Well, yes. But she's back in her own room now. You don't have to worry about it. You can go back to sleep."

"But what was the matter?"

"DTs. Now please go to sleep."

That made some kind of sense out of it, and I did what she told me.

When I opened my eyes, it was day. A group of young doctors were in the room making their morning rounds. I listened to them joke about something, then as they examined my chart I turned to the one who seemed to be in charge.

"Look, can I talk to my doctor?"

He smiled patronizingly. The others followed his lead.

"Well, your doctor will come see you."

"When?"

"Soon."

"Can I call him on the phone?"

I had noticed there was no telephone in the room.

"No, no. He'll be around."

Everything was very vague. I could see I wasn't going

to get any information out of him. That's how it is in those places.

A hypodermic needle was drawing fluid out of a small bottle.

"Hey, wait a minute. You can't give me a shot until I talk to my doctor. I've got to talk to my doctor."

The smiles faded, and they tensed ever so slightly. They had been here before.

"Look, miss. Your doctor has prescribed this medication."

More forcefully now.

"And you are going to take it."

"I don't want to."

"Well, you have a choice. Either we can hold you down and give you the shot, or you can sit up and let us give you the shot."

Pause.

"Which is it going to be?"

Some choice.

The next time I woke up it was late afternoon and my doctor was there in the room. When I asked him what was going to happen, he was very kind and understanding and also very vague. I wanted to get out of there. I didn't know where I could go—certainly not back to the theater—but I didn't want to be there. The place scared me.

He shook his head and said, "No, Elizabeth, you're not ready to leave yet. I don't know how long you'll have to stay here. We have to find out what the problem is."

A rush of paranoia flashed through me. Maybe they didn't want me to get out of here.

"Uh, has anybody talked to the producer?"

"Everyone's been told you were hospitalized."

I felt myself wince.

24

"Don't worry. They think you have a bronchial infection."

A bronchial infection? Fine. Okay.

"Now you ought to get some more rest."

I lay there I don't know how many days, drifting in and out of consciousness. Every so often my doctor would come around and ask me questions. I could never answer them.

"Do you want to see George?"

George had called him from California. He was anxious to come see me. I really didn't want him to, not while I was like this, but I was afraid to say so. He was the only person who cared at all what happened to me. But an honest answer would have been too complicated to handle.

All I could say was, "I don't know."

"Well, do you want to go back to the show?"

"I don't know."

The only thing I was sure about was wanting to get out of there.

"Couldn't I go home instead? Have a nurse and get well at home? In my own bed, with a nurse?"

"No, that's not how it works. You're either inside here or you're out there. You can't have it both ways."

"If I go out there, then I have to go back and do what I was supposed to do?"

"Yes."

"Then I guess I'll have to stay here."

I didn't know what else to do. I didn't know how to be inside. I didn't know how to be outside. Being inside was like capitulating to destiny. I had always felt that some part of my destiny was madness. I'd grown up with my grandmother and watched her turn into Crazy Nanny. But if I went outside, I had to do everything I had already tried to do and failed at. I couldn't take the re-sponsibility of letting everybody down again.

The only choice was madness.

But I knew I was only faking it. I knew I was just tired and scared and confused and unable to do whatever it was I had somehow promised to do. Yet it was either be a star, this impossible Golden Girl, or be crazy. No contest. Crazy was easier.

But I was counterfeit. The truly peculiar thing was that I had gone in there because I felt counterfeit, and once I was in there I was also counterfeit. Counterfeit star. Counterfeit crazy. I couldn't get away from it.

I settled in and spent my days in bed reading movie magazines. Every so often an attendant would come in with a tray of food. There were never any utensils, only a plastic spoon they made sure to take away when I finished.

But even here total escape wasn't possible. Your door always stayed open—you weren't allowed to close it —and the hall was filled with a constant parade of pa-tients. They weren't just passing through. I came to realize that most of them were there quite a lot. They lived there. And they would walk into your room without thinking twice. At first I would say to them, "No, no, not now. I'd like to be alone, please." But that was like waving a red flag in front of a bull. I was the new one they hadn't seen before, and if you are new you are fair game. So they would stroll in and look at you and giggle and laugh and point—because they were all crazy! It finally started to get through to me that I was in a fucking crazy house and everyone here was nuts!

An immensely fat woman shuffled into my room and plopped herself down on the chair. She had about three teeth in her head and looked sixty, although she was probably about forty.

With a conspiratorial wink, she started in on me.

"Listen, wanna know who I really am?"

"What?"

"Wanna know who I really am? I'm really Alexander the Great. Thass right. I was Alexander the Great in my previous incarnation. No kiddin'."

Alexander the Great. Jesus, I thought that was just in the funny papers.

"Oh, really?"

(What else do you say?)

"Thass right. I have it documented. I did tape recordings. But I can't get anybody to listen to them."

She launched into her story about how the history books were all wrong and deliberately suppressing the truth; and after detailing what she was going to do about it, she raised herself up and just as suddenly as she came in she was gone.

The next time the nurse came through I told her I had to talk to her.

"Look, I know I'm here because the doctor put me here and I have to stay until he says I can go. But really, I've got to get on another floor or something. Because" —and I found myself saying it just like all the others— "because, you don't understand, I AM NOT CRAZY!"

I knew what she was going to say before the words left her mouth.

"Of course. You talk to your doctor. Of course."

I had to break through.

"Hey, wait a minute. Listen, I don't think I'm Alexander the Great! I'm not jumping around like I have St. Vitus's dance at four o'clock in the morning! I mean, get me a phone!"

The more I tried to reach her, the more insane I sounded.

"Listen, please, please! Go get a *Life* magazine! I'm

on the cover! I shouldn't be here! I'm Elizabeth Ashley!"
Sure, sure you are.

A few days later I received an unexpected visit from
my old pal Doc.

"Hi!" he chirped as he wafted in. "I came to see who
was here. I heard there was some kind of star. I didn't
know it was *you!*"

The year before, Doc and I both lived in the same
bizarro apartment house in Hell's Kitchen. It was a kennel
full of fruitcakes. Leather queens. A clique of crazy alcoholic junkies who worked at the New York Public Library.
An aristocratic lawyer dying of some strange disease. His
black boy trick, a Forty-second Street whore who glided
around the building in royal robes. What do you want for
your eighty-five bucks a month?

Doc was a Southern, seriously alcoholic doctor. The
people in the building who were into pills all scored
their stuff off of him. Every week he got drunk, went
down to Times Square and picked up dangerous street
trade—sailors and heavy-leather guys. He'd bring them
home, and they would beat him up and take his money.
Sometimes the beatings got so bad he'd run down to my
place screaming. If I had any friends hanging out with
me, we would chase the trick out of there. Often when I
came home at night I would find Doc asleep in the doorway, too drunk to climb the stairs. I'd try to carry him
up, then jimmy open the lock to his apartment and put
him to bed. He had one room. The whole place was filled
with a Catholic altar and a cot.

"Doc! Jesus Christ, what are you doing here?"

"I work here, hon. Not on this floor. This is the
heavy-security floor. But downstairs."

Thank God, I thought. At least there is one person

here who knows me from the outside. I saw him immediately as my connection to the, so to speak, real world.

"Doc, I've got to get a telephone."

He looked at me and shook his head.

"Uh-uh. There's a pay phone out there in the recreation room, but that's the only phone you're going to get. And they won't let you stay on it very long. Hon, you're on the floor the elevator doesn't stop at."

"What do I do?"

"Well, talk to your doctor about that. Just get all the rest you can and talk to your doctor."

"I've got to start making some sense with these staff people."

"You can't. Everything they're doing is straight from your doctor, so that's who you have to talk to if you want anything changed."

So that was that.

About two weeks later George flew in from California. He had spoken with the doctor and the producer of my show and laid it all out for me. The deal hadn't changed. It was still the same.

"It's up to you when you want to go home. But when you do go home, then you will have to come to terms with the realities. There is a contract, Elizabeth. They want you in the play. And you are going to have to deal with that."

The attitude about me was that I had had a temper tantrum because I wanted to get out of the show. And it was, okay, this is where "out" is. Now, is this what you want? Or do you want to pull up your socks, get off the dime, be a good girl and go back to work?

I felt foolish and stupid because the point they were making was: You're not crazy. You think you're crazy?

You're copping out. It was like I was a bad child who had gotten caught playing hooky, and that had always been my worst nightmare. From the time I was a kid I had never been able to show up. I could never cut it. And now it had come true again in the one place where I had ever been accepted. I still couldn't cut it, and I still didn't know why.

I thought it over a few minutes, then very quietly, but with a vengeance, gave him my answer.

"Right. I will go back to the show, be a good girl, and do as I'm told."

George handed me some dimes. I went to the pay phone and made the calls. And the next week I did go back, meek as a lamb.

I was in my dressing room putting on my makeup for the first time in a month when Mike Nichols, the director on the show, came in to say hello.

I looked at him through the mirror and decided to tell him the truth.

"Mike, I've got to tell you something. I didn't have a bronchial infection. I was in Payne Whitney. And I don't feel like I know any more now than I did before I went in there. I don't know if I'm going to go crazy again or what."

I can still remember his words.

"Listen to me, Bessie. I've been in the nut house. Everybody I know has been in the nut house. It's not something that makes you better. It's the last resort when you can't take it any more."

He put his hand on my shoulder, and I turned around to face him directly.

"Look at me," he said. "I'm still crazy. I never know from one day to the next if I'm going to be able to make it. Come on. You're wonderful. Get on with it."

30

I'll never forget him for that.

He made me feel that I wasn't alone. That I wasn't a leper. That I wasn't the only person in the world who couldn't always cut it.

But in my heart of hearts I also heard another voice that said, "Yeah, Mike. But you're talented. And you're intelligent. And you're real. You're a real person, and I'm only counterfeit."

I will never know for sure whether or not I was actually crazy. Maybe no one ever does. All you come out of that with is a sense of failure because you could no longer deliver. And for me, it wasn't as if I ever got cured. It was just that finally I had no choice but to function or be locked up with the burden of that guilt forever. The bottom line was either to die or to do, and I picked to do because I was scared to die.

But there was nothing noble in that. It was, all right, I'll say anything you want me to say, pretend to be anybody you want me to pretend I am. I will fake the rules. And I just hope to God they don't get too hard. I'm not going to search for answers. I am just going to try to stand up on my feet and not get put away again.

Hollywood, 1963

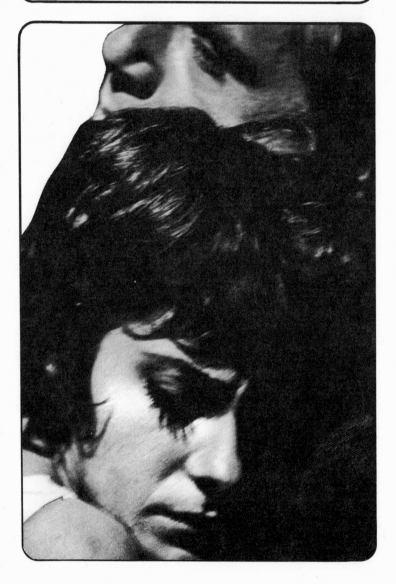

2

Earlier that year, while Neil Simon was writing *Barefoot in the Park* for me, I went to California to become a movie star. Two years and three pictures later I quit acting altogether and ran away with my tail between my legs to become a Beverly Hills housewife.

I was brought to Hollywood by Marty Rackin, the head of production at Paramount. He had seen me on Broadway in *Take Her, She's Mine* and wanted me for *The Carpetbaggers,* which they were just starting to cast. I had to test for the part, but I knew I had it, mostly because Marty Rackin wanted me to have it. He pushed me on Joe Levine, the producer of the picture. Levine didn't really care. He already had Carroll Baker, who got to take off her clothes. It didn't much matter who the other broads were.

Rackin knew I was good casting, even though I was so skinny they had to pad me out to give me a proper Hollywood body. I had started out and made it in comedy, and the girl I played was the only character with any funny lines. To this day, people who don't know me from anything else come up to me on the street and tell me they still remember one line I had in that movie. My fiancé says to me, "What do you want to see on your honeymoon?" and I answer, "Lots of lovely ceilings."

Marty Rackin was the reason I got to say that kind of dialogue. He understood that, if anything, I was a throwback to the kind of ballsy, smart-mouthed women who were in the movies in the 1930s. I'm certain he also knew I would walk off with the picture. He never said it, but anybody who could read could have told you from the script that whoever played the part was going to be the one who got the notices.

Marty Rackin was a real Damon Runyon character and one of the best people I ever knew in the movie business. I loved Marty Rackin. He was a man you could talk to.

During filming I would do things like go running into his office and say, "I'm hiding in the bathroom so Nellie Manley won't get me!" Nellie Manley was a terrific hair stylist who had done all the marcel waves on Dietrich back in the thirties, and now she was doing Carroll Baker, Martha Hyer, and me on *Carpetbaggers*. I wanted to wear my hair absolutely straight so that it moved with me, but not a lot of people had moving hair in pictures then. Rackin laughed and said, "Listen, I'll fight city hall for ya, but I ain't fightin' Nellie Manley. So you just hide in the bathroom and handle it any way you can."

Rackin dealt with me like a New York City street kid. It was always, "Listen, kid, keep your mouth shut and put on a dress and you'll do okay." He believed I was going to be a movie star. I believed it too.

I had just come from a Tony Award on Broadway and now I had *Carpetbaggers,* a Big Movie. I was hot and I knew I was hot, and I understood how that could get parlayed. I realized that you had to get into certain pictures and be brought along a certain way and that it didn't always go down the way it was supposed to. But I had Marty Rackin in my corner. He liked me, and liked me pretty much for what I was. I think he saw in me what there was to see and knew what my appeal would be.

I remember him saying, "Kid, you're as good-lookin' as Audrey Hepburn. Neither one of you has any tits. But you're a lot tougher and meaner and dirtier." That's how he would sum me up to people on the telephone: "It's a dirty Audrey Hepburn." And that was something I was perfectly capable of being. I didn't have to stretch for that one at all.

I was skinny and angular and dark, with huge eyes, a funny voice, and a fast, dirty mouth. I wore my hair cut short like a boy and used hardly any makeup. The girls my age who were comers then were Sandra Dee, Ann-Margret, and Yvette Mimieux, and I certainly didn't fit into that golden-haired mold. When I went to hair and makeup for my test, they took one look at me and said, "You would make a terrific blonde." The thinking was still that anybody who could be should be. "Twenty years ago," Rackin told me, "you wouldn't have gotten dick in this town."

I'm sure that was true, but this was the early sixties. The fifties were finally over, and the feeling was there had to be something besides Sandra Dee. Maybe it would be me. It wasn't as if I were some kid from Hollywood down on her knees trying to score any kind of miracle or break. Coming from New York still had a certain amount of clout to it, especially if they thought you were good-looking enough for the movies.

I had flown out four or five times before to do some small television parts, but that was entirely different. You checked in at the Montecito Hotel, that Hollywood ghetto full of New York actors pretending they're still on West Forty-fifth Street. You did your television gig. Then you got on the Red Eye Special and flew back to New York. But this was the Big Time. In the early sixties there was no slopover between movies and television. Movie people didn't even know who television people were. And if you scored a big part in a movie, you learned very fast to play down anything you had done on television because that would immediately lower your stock.

My picture was also in a lot of fashion magazines. The

sort of chic world was saying, "This is an interesting-looking kid and her action is a little different from every-body else's." That also impressed them, and I was per-fectly aware of how to play it to the hilt.

I had always known that my only chance in anything was to emphasize the difference between myself and every-one else. I never got anywhere trying to be the same. So as flat-chested as I was, I made myself look even more flat-chested. I went totally against the stereotyped sexuality of the girls in the movies, which had never been my kind of sexuality to begin with. I didn't have big tits, and I could never play the role of supplicant to the man. Do-to-me-whatever-you-want-to-do-to-me-honey had just never been my style. I also knew that on my own turf I was sexier in jeans, a T-shirt, no makeup, and my hair cut off than most of the chicks with the big tits, pushup bras, and flowing locks. To be sure, the minute I went on to other people's turf I couldn't get to first base. Yet a lot of men in town were hitting on me, and it was obvious that what they liked about me was not what was being served up as sex appeal by the movies.

I learned quickly to be careful about that one. One of the first pieces of advice given me when I came to Holly-wood was, "Don't date." My manager, Bullets Durgom, knew that game and those people very well. He explained to me that Hollywood is a town full of guys with their jaws hanging down for the new meat on the market. "And you get used up real fast," he told me. "Even if you don't screw them, even if you just go to dinner with five of them, you have been had. So don't date. Stick to yourself." Or best of all, do what I was already doing. I was already involved with George Peppard, who was a hot actor, and they all liked that just fine. It couldn't have been better. It meant that I got in the papers because he got in the papers. Every time he would be mentioned I would be mentioned, and since we were both in *Carpetbaggers,* the publicity was good for selling the picture.

It also meant that I was not available and no one could have me. In those days that was the secret for being a lady movie star. If you were going to make it big as an actress in film, it was a matter of who couldn't have you rather than who could. But you had to have a legitimate reason for not being had so that you were not in the position of rejecting the high rollers. Because then they would get mad at you and say, "Over my dead body. That bitch will never work for me."

And yet you had to turn them on. They had to have that sexual fantasy about you, and they weren't wrong. If you are supposed to be someone everyone in the world wants to screw, there had better be a lot of people who do in fact want to screw you. And the only way a man has of being certain about that is if he wants to perform the deed himself.

The week I signed with Paramount, Marty Rackin gave a cocktail party for me at his home, a huge Tudor mansion down in the flats of Beverly Hills. On the drive over, George briefed me about what to expect and made me promise to behave myself. As we left his apartment, I looked for the funky old trenchcoat I always wore, but he had hidden it. I had on a boyish, rather stark black-and-white linen dress designed by Donald Brooks that emphasized how tall and skinny I was. I didn't wear any jewelry or makeup, except for my eyes. When we walked into Rackin's front door, he checked me up and down, then laughed and said, "Would you look at you, would you look at you! I thought you'd at least put on some falsies!"

There must have been three hundred people there,

all the heavyweights in the industry—"our industry," as they do love to call it—from John Wayne to Louella Parsons. Parsons was very old and sick by then. She had had a stroke and could hardly speak. They sat her down in a chair on a plastic pillow, where she reigned over the proceedings like a queen, framed between the Utrillo and the Grandma Moses. A platoon of uniformed Mexicans maneuvered around the room with platters of tarted up bagels and tacos. There was lots and lots of booze.

The style was casual—Jax outfits on the women and sportclothes on the men—but behind the suntans and chit-chat everyone was working hard. I watched the actors who were playing the game make the rounds of the executives. Even those who were considerably older than some of the executives were treated like boys and slapped on the back rather too familiarly when they came up to pay their respects. The boys and their ladies made a point of playing up to the executives' wives.

No one particularly wanted to be there. They were all grown-up people with better things to do. But the party was being given by the head of a studio and it would be in the papers the next day. The real purpose of a party like that is to be seen. It means that you are included, which is confirmation that your stock is steady or rising and you have not fallen from grace. The only ways they had of knowing who had fallen from grace and who hadn't were by who showed up, whose name was in the paper, and who was able to make a deal. That's the way it was measured then and probably still is.

On the surface it was all very friendly and family-like. They talked about their kids. They talked about their paintings. They talked about their cars. They talked about salads. The wives of the executives tell you where to go to get the best vegetables and the best butcher. And you listen, even though you suspect it's all window dressing, all makeup and hair. That was the particular Hollywood style of that time. Behind your back in the office, or on the telephone with agents, they could be brutal, but there would never be any one-on-one confrontation, the way there is in New York. In the New York theater everyone is carrying his long knife right out in front of him, so you know what to expect. Yet peculiarly enough, behind your back they might be pretty decent.

I had no illusions about what was going on, other than the standard New York stage actor's prejudices about Hollywood. It had been drilled into me that they were all imbeciles, they all did garbage, they all lived materialistic, empty lives. The usual ill-informed caricature. I was surprised that some of the people I met were really quite bright and interesting. There were a couple of old comedy writers there, and we had a good time trading smart mouth back and forth. Then I remember listening to Henry Hathaway, the director, talk with George about a picture they had done together and thinking, well, this is a fine, salty old dude. He didn't have the same kind of glassy-eyed rap as most everyone else.

That's when I made my one slip of the evening. Hathaway said something I liked, and I let loose with a "Fucking A!" George frowned, then took me aside.

"Hey, I told you never to talk that way."

"Oh, come on. Why not?"

"Because they don't like to hear that coming from ladies."

Later on he explained to me once again that to have sex appeal in the movies, which is what a woman primarily had to have, you didn't talk dirty, you never discussed sex, and you were never one of the boys. You always kept yourself a little remote. I promised I would try to remember.

Marty Rackin took me around and introduced me to

all the people it was important for me to meet. Everyone was terribly nice. I was an unknown quantity out to make a big picture, and you are never hotter than right before you have actually done something. Nobody really knows anything about you. Nobody's even seen you on the screen yet. But you might be the one; you might be the one. So for all their power they are afraid not to kiss your ass. But on the other hand, there will be nineteen others like you who are going to be brought out the same way that year, and out of twenty asses to kiss only one will be remembered in twelve months.

The introductions followed a certain stylized code. People were introduced with their credits, but in an oblique sort of way. It wasn't as direct as, "This is Joe Shmoe, the president of Columbia Pictures, who is going to be deciding the casting on this movie you might be really right for." The way it went was, "Joe Shmoe, meet Elizabeth Ashley. You better be nice to her because when you want to talk to her about such-and-such a project I may have her tied up." A little joke, which you were supposed to be savvy enough to get. Oh yeah, he's got this property and I may want to do it, so I better try to lay in an instant impression.

I was only twenty-two years old, but I had come from New York and had some pretty good street smarts for a kid. I realized right away I could never compete in that arena if I stuck to the rules. My best move would be not to play the game at all. And if I do say so myself, I knew how to not play the game brilliantly.

Rackin would make his introduction and I'd say, "Excuse me, but I didn't understand any of that. I mean, where do you work? What do you do? I'm from New York, man. I just came in from Greenwich Village. You could be the highest roller in this town, and I wouldn't know. But if you are, give me a break and tell me, will you?"

And many of them would. They were charmed. I

knew I would only be able to get along with the people I was able to disarm. Being in the position of supplicant was intolerable to me. Everything in my spirit fought against it. I also knew the only way to be heard was never to merchandise what I had to say in order to score a job. People out there dealt with well meaning, self serving bullshit every day of their lives.

The party ended about nine. I stuck around for a while to find out how I did. I was a hit. Louella had stayed the whole three hours.

I thought it was going to be easy.

I was wrong.

After *Carpetbaggers* was finished, I went back to New York to start rehearsing *Barefoot in the Park*. The show was a big success, and I played it for close to a year. Then I returned to Hollywood to make *Ship of Fools* for Columbia.

When I had signed with Paramount, my managers had negotiated with Marty Rackin what is known as a multiple picture nonexclusive contract, which was absolutely the best sort of contract a young actor could have. It meant that I was committed to Paramount for something like a picture a year for five years on a graduated pay scale, but they did not own me. They had first call, but I could work anywhere else in whatever way I chose. When *Ship of Fools* came up, I really owed Paramount my second movie, and Otto Preminger wanted me for something he was producing there. But Marty Rackin knew that *Ship of Fools* would be a much better career move for me, even though it was for a rival studio. It was adapted from Katharine Anne Porter's very good, best-selling novel and was to be produced and directed by Stanley Kramer with a cast that included heavyweights like Vivien Leigh, Simone Signoret, Oskar Werner, Jose

Ferrer, and Lee Marvin. Rackin also knew I didn't want to work with Preminger. For an actor, that would be like getting sent off to be beaten and stoned. Somehow he politicked it through for me and got Paramount to defer my commitment.

When I completed *Ship of Fools* I ran off to Europe for six months. I wasn't at all happy with my work in the picture and didn't want to stick around while it was being edited. While I was gone, there was a turnover at Paramount, and the gossip was the new board of directors at Gulf and Western gave Marty Rackin the ax. The news took me totally by surprise. I didn't realize that the production head of a studio is a highly paid scapegoat who is always the first to go when a new regime comes in. It's one of the most harrowing jobs in the world. You're lucky if you can hold on for two or three years.

I came back from Europe to do a turkey called *The Third Day* for Warner Brothers. I could tell from the script it was going to be a piece of technicolor garbage, but I would be costarring with George. My agents, who were also George's agents, thought it was a good idea and pressured me to make it. It would be a big commercial movie. My name would be above the title, which would make me a real leading lady. I would earn a lot of money. I had been paid twenty thousand for *Carpetbaggers* and fifty thousand for *Ship of Fools*. For this one I would get a hundred. This is the way you run a career, they explained. *Ship of Fools* was still being edited, so I had been off the screen for a while, and the important thing at this point was to maintain momentum.

While I was finishing up *The Third Day*, I had to start thinking about meeting my Paramount commitment. I knew I had better do something good. Then a script came to me called *Cross Your Heart and Hope to Die*. It was written by Sterling Silliphant, an excellent screen writer, and was to costar Sidney Poitier, who also had a deal at Paramount. The picture was about the workings of a suicide prevention center. No one at the studio thought it would make much money, but they were willing to go ahead with it if it could be done for under a million dollars. Even though Poitier had won an Academy Award the year before, word was that he still couldn't carry a picture. I was hot in the business, but not all that well known outside it.

When I said I would do it, the usual announcements were made to the trade. A lot of people tried to talk me out of it: "What do you want to do that for? It's depressing. It's down." But I thought it would be a good movie. The subject interested me. The script was good. I didn't know Poitier well, but I liked him and wanted to work with him.

When it came time to sign a director, I brought pressure on Paramount through my managers and agents and everybody else I knew to give the job to Sydney Pollack. Sydney had been one of my teachers at the Neighborhood Playhouse, then had gone on to become a television director. He had never directed a feature film, but he was excellent with actors and I was getting very insecure about my acting. Everyone was telling me how good I was, but I didn't think I was good.

Paramount agreed to give Sydney a shot, and we were thrilled that we had finessed this score and would be working together. I liked him. I trusted him. I thought he could help me. We would start shooting in a couple of months, just as soon as Poitier finished up another project. Meanwhile, I began working at a suicide prevention center, listening in on the calls, talking with the doctors and reading the books they recommended. I was feeling strong and good.

Then I went to the screening of *Ship of Fools.*

George was working in London, so I drove over to Columbia by myself. Just about everyone who had worked on the film was there. Stanley Kramer. Simone Signoret, Jose Ferrer, Oskar Werner, and the other actors. The crew and their wives. This was the first time we were all back together since the end of shooting, and the screening room was filled with lots of big hellos and high-spirited kidding around. None of us had seen it yet, but the word from the studio was that it was terrific. I'd had some concern about my performance, but they assured me I was wonderful. What did I know? It was only my second film.

The lights went down and the movie began.

When I saw my work up on the screen I was appalled. It was terrible—cheap, histrionic, first-year acting-school acting. And I knew why. I had been so intimidated by being in that cast that I had gone against all my instincts and done everything Stanley Kramer told me to do. After breaking down in *Barefoot in the Park,* I was trying to clean up my act, be a good girl, and do it right. And now here it was. There was no subtlety. No reality. It was all put-up, hype acting.

We had rehearsed the movie for two weeks before starting to shoot. When you first go into rehearsal in a play, you either overdo everything or underdo everything. I always tend to do too much, so the rehearsal period becomes a process of paring down for me. But I never got to do that with Kramer. He kept saying, "That's what I want! That's what I want!" My instincts told me what he was asking me to do was cheap and wrong and bad. But I knew if I resisted I could be considered difficult and have to fight for my ideas in front of all the high rollers in the cast. And I didn't have the courage to do that. I was intimidated by them and was afraid to make any waves. So what I got was a lot of popularity on the set— they all thought I was just terrific—and shit on the screen forever. Forever. Hysterical, fake, empty bullshit.

It wouldn't have been so devastating if I had gone for something I believed in. I still would have been humiliated and horrified, but I wouldn't have felt so cheap. Because I knew that my big problem as a performer is the need for instant gratification. I want to please whoever is there. That's why I'm better on the stage than I am on a movie set. The audience keeps me straight.

I slumped down in my seat, overcome with embarrassment and shame. It started in my stomach, came up and got me by the throat, and then I covered my eyes and was unable to look.

And I knew it wasn't just seeing myself up on the screen for the second time in my life. Usually people will talk and joke and carry on at that kind of screening, but whenever one of my scenes came up there was dead silence. I sneaked a look at some of the faces in the audience. When I happened to catch someone's eye, he would turn away from me.

The absolute worst was two scenes I played with George Segal, where Kramer had wanted me to get especially overt, big, and hysterical. I had thought I should be much more laid back than that, but George Segal played everything very low, so Kramer had to get me up to compensate.

The way the sequence was written, it begins with my getting drunk in the ship's bar and flirting with a troupe of Spanish gypsies. Then Segal, who played my boyfriend, comes in and starts an argument with me, which escalates into a physical fight. At the end of the scene he takes a hard swing at me and hits me in the face. Then there is a cut to the next scene, which shows the two of us in bed.

Well, as is often the way in the movies, we shot the scene in bed before the scene with the gypsies. Since I was supposed to have just come off having been slugged by him, that's the way I played it. And the more nothing

Segal did, the more Kramer got me yelling and screaming and chewing the scenery.

When we finished shooting that day and I told George
how it had gone, he said, "Watch that one, babe. Watch
that. They'll do it to you. Columbia doesn't have a deal
with you. They have a deal with Segal. He's the one who's
going to get the protection. You better protect yourself."

I didn't know about protecting myself. I trusted
Stanley Kramer. If that's what Stanley Kramer wanted,
that's what I was going to give him. Unquestioningly. Like
a lemming.

A week later we started shooting the beginning of the
scene in the bar with me and the gypsies. We would do
George Segal and me the next day. I had to be blatant
enough to irk Segal into hitting me because it was all
aimed at him. The point of the scene was that the man
couldn't get it up and the girlfriend couldn't take it any
more that he couldn't get it up, so she says, in effect,
"Okay, you won't fuck me? They will." The psychology
was clear. You provoke the man so that if he won't screw
you, he will at least fight you. So I really went for it. My
training is that you always work with the other actor. If
you are supposed to provoke him to hit you, you've got to
give him something to get him to do that.

The next morning when we came to the part where
George Segal and I have the fight, he turned to Stanley
Kramer and said, "Stanley, I'm not gonna hit her."

It didn't make any sense. I had played the top of that
scene and the beginning of the next completely based
on the fact that I would be hit. That was the only way I
could justify what Kramer was asking me to do. He kept
telling me, "Remember, you get beaten up."

There was a moment of silence, then Kramer said,
"What?" and Segal said it again. "I'm not gonna hit her,
Stanley. I wouldn't hit her."

46

I was told later that Segal's wife had said, "George, don't hit the character. It doesn't look good. You won't be a leading man, George, if you hit her." And Stanley Kramer couldn't seem to get him to do it, either. So what ended up on the screen, is this hysterical, wide-open, scenery-chewing bullshit which is utterly meaningless and has nothing to do with anything else that is going on.

The picture finally ended, and I got out of the screening room before the lights came up. On the drive home all I could think was, "I'm going to have to redeem myself. I am going to have to redeem myself." I usually operate right off of my prejudices and defenses, but I knew this was more important than that. I wasn't mad at Stanley Kramer. I wasn't mad at George Segal. I wasn't mad at anybody but myself because I hadn't even tried to fight against what I instinctively knew was wrong. I had been too much of a coward to risk being called foolish or difficult.

I let myself into my apartment, then went straight to the telephone and called George in London. He said, "Well, you're probably just reacting to seeing yourself on the screen. Don't say anything to anybody. Not a word."

I should have listened to him. I didn't. George always gave me good advice, but I was never comfortable with it because he didn't like my being an actress. That was the big bone of contention between us. As far as he was concerned, actresses were all sick, fucked-up women, so as soon as I had a problem that's what I was behaving like. I would argue with him, "I'm not sick and fucked up. I can be your old lady and an actress too. I can handle them both." Well, you really can't, but you go crazy finding that one out. So the one person I was closest to was the last person I would listen to, because his attitude would finally be, "I told you so." Which is what happened

47

that night. Ten minutes into the conversation he was saying, "I told you not to do that part anyway. Why did you want to be in that picture in the first place? It was a no-win situation."

We hung up, and I immediately dialed Sydney Pollack and made a date to have lunch with him the next day. I realized it was too late to do anything about *Ship of Fools,* but I could still redeem myself on *Cross My Heart and Hope to Die.* Sydney and I had never been tight buddies, but he'd been one of my acting teachers and I did put all the politics and muscle in motion to get him the job.

We met at a little restaurant on Melrose where everybody at Paramount went to lunch. I let it all out and told him the absolute truth.

"Sydney, you're going to have to help me. I'm going to need a lot of help. I've just seen *Ship of Fools,* and I'm terrible in it. I hate what I did. I wasn't strong enough to fight for what was right. I don't know any more if I even remember the proper way to work. You're going to have to help me, Sydney. You're going to have to ride me. You're going to have to make me do what's right."

He asked a lot of questions, then tried to make me feel better.

"Well, why don't you wait until *Ship of Fools* comes out? It's probably not all that bad."

I said, "Sydney, I am that bad. I wish that Kramer would just cut me out of it."

A week later I returned home from the suicide prevention center and found Sydney waiting for me in the lobby.

"Hi, Sydney, what's happening?"

I had never seen him so nervous and upset. When I took his hand it was clammy and unsteady.

We went upstairs, and I asked him, "Well, what is it? Whatever it is, it can't be that bad." I thought he had run into some kind of trouble with the film and needed my help.

He said, "I've got to have a drink. Do you have any liquor around?"

I found a bottle of gin. He poured himself a large glass and drank it down straight. Finally he was ready to talk.

"I don't know how to tell you, but you're out of the picture."

"What do you mean?"

I wasn't upset. I just didn't understand what he was saying.

He said it again.

"You're out of the picture. They've replaced you. All I know is they told me today it's going to Anne Bancroft."

"Sydney, that's not possible. It's been announced. I have a commitment with Paramount."

He sat there staring into his glass. I kept waiting for him to say, "So I told them I'm not doing it either." At which point I would have answered, "Sydney, don't be silly." That's how that one is supposed to go. But Sydney didn't say that.

The room seemed to change. Something in me pulled back, and it all looked very distant and unfamiliar. It was as if I were no longer there.

I said, "Okay, Sydney. Let me see what my agents know about it. I'll be talking to you."

He left, and I made the call. My agents weren't too informed about it either and would have to get back to me. I sat by the telephone for the next two hours chain-smoking and trying to figure out what was going on. It seemed to take forever, but the phone finally rang.

The story seemed to go like this: A few days after Sydney and I met for lunch, the board of directors held a meeting in New York to approve the budgets for all the upcoming pictures. They agreed to go with *Cross My Heart and Hope to Die* only if it could be made for under a million dollars, but Sydney and the producer had been up on locations in Seattle and now the budget was coming in closer to one and a half million. The board's response was, "Well now, for one-five we have Sidney Poitier and Elizabeth Ashley, but Poitier can't carry, and who is Ashley?" Then a mysterious someone supposedly pulled out a photograph of Anne Bancroft handing Poitier the Academy Award, which she had won the year before. One of the board was supposed to have said, "Well, why not put Bancroft in it? Maybe two Academy Award winners could justify the extra five hundred thousand."

The bottom line was that I was indeed fired. It had already been announced that I would be doing the picture, so to all appearances that meant they were firing me for incompetence, even though I had not yet shot a foot of film.

I was stunned. I needed some time to process what they told me, so we set up a meeting for the next morning that would include my manager. I was just a kid. I didn't know much about anything. But by the time I walked into the office I had made up my mind about what I had to do.

"I am going to sue them," I said. "There must be grounds for a lawsuit, and that's what I want. They are damaging me professionally and artistically and putting my reputation in jeopardy. I'm being fired before I've even started. They can't humiliate and denigrate me like this. I may never recover from it. I am not a piece of meat. I want my contract to be null and void. And I want an apology. I don't want to work for those people.

They're not the ones I made the contract with anyway, and if this is the way the new regime is, the hell with it!"

My manager said, "If that's what you want, Elizabeth, I'm sure they will let you out of your contract without going to court. They don't want a lawsuit."

"They don't want a lawsuit?" I yelled. "That's what they're going to get. I don't want any gifts from them. I don't want good will with them. I want due process of law. That's the only way I'll be able to get the information and find out why this has happened to me."

Someone said, "If you play it right, they'll probably come up with some bucks. Lawsuits don't look good to boards of directors."

I couldn't be talked out of it.

"I do not want money," I told them. "It's not a matter of money. It's a matter of principle."

The moment I mentioned "principle" eyes darted across the room and they pulled away from me like I had suddenly broken out in a smell.

Over the next few weeks the phone calls started coming in from the Wiser Advisors in the business.

"That's not the way to run a career."

"We do not sue major studios. We deal with them."

"They'll get you another picture. They'll give you a lot of money."

"Don't be mad. That's childish. It's better to play ball."

I could no more play ball than I could sprout wings and fly to the moon. I don't have that in me.

"Fuck playing ball! Are you telling me I may never work again?"

"Oh, no, no, no. I never said that."

51

"Well, if that is what you're telling me, then I won't work again! But I am going to sue those bastards."

There were also some calls of an entirely different sort from a few people rather high up in the industry. They sounded almost as if they were speaking from pay phones. I was never to call them at their offices. There was to be no record we ever talked.

"If you are going to pursue this, protect yourself, kid," one of them confided. "Stay away from California show-business lawyers. They all owe lots more slices of their ass to the movie companies than they do to you."

I had just been appointed to the National Council on the Arts, so I phoned one of my government friends in Washington and asked him to get me an attorney. He came up with a California firm called Gibson, Dunne and Crutcher, which was about as WASP, snob, high rent, and right wing as they get. It was the same law firm with which one Richard Nixon had practiced law. The closest to show business they had ever come was representing CBS on something, but they agreed to take the case because it wasn't about money but about ethics, the question of an artist's rights.

It turned out that the Paramount legal department had screwed up badly. The studio had fired me on the assumption that they had a pay-or-play clause with me. If they did, they would have been within their rights to take me off the picture and either pay me off or stick me in something else. But because of a good contract negotiated when I was hot, they did not have that right. And that meant Paramount *really* didn't want to go to court. The thrust of my suit was that they had dealt with me in a reprehensible, immoral way. Not only were they in breach, but they were in breach because of their lack of ethics. The board of directors from Gulf and Western weren't people who were used to the movies, and it reinforced everything they suspected about movie people, that they're all kind of scuzzy and eighth-rate.

I had them and had them good.

Then I read the depositions at my lawyers' office, and it took all the fight out of me. They read me the statements from Sydney Pollack; from Howard Koch, the new head of production; from Stephen Alexander, the producer of the picture; and from a lot of the people at the William Morris office, which represented both Pollack and Bancroft.

I found out that after having lunch with me, Sydney Pollack went straight to his agents at William Morris and said something like, "Christ, I've just been with Ashley, and she's scared to death. She said she saw *Ship of Fools* and she's shitty in it, and now she's afraid she can't do my picture. What are we going to do?"

I found out that the William Morris Agency may have induced Paramount to breach. Anne Bancroft, who is very much a class actress, needed some money and wanted a movie job, but the Morris office wasn't able to get her one. Then one of the agents pulled out the glossy of Miss Bancroft handing the Academy Award to Mr. Poitier, and a bright idea was born.

"The movie is going to come in for over a million dollars anyway, isn't it?"

"Mmmm-mmm, yeah. Sure."

"Fine."

Someone from the Morris office in New York went to the board of directors meeting and said, "Listen, you've got Sydney Poitier, who cannot carry, and you've got Elizabeth Ashley, who's scared to death and we understand from inside information is shit in *Ship of Fools*. Now take her out of it, stick Bancroft in, and at least you'll have Bancroft and Poitier. Put the two of them together, and maybe you'll get as good as one."

53

I found out that Sterling Silliphant, with whom I had spent many hours going over the script, was one of the first to say, "Sure, dump her."

I found out that the day Howard Koch assured me at lunch that everything was fine, he had just been on the phone with William Morris making Anne Bancroft's negotiations.

By the time I finished the depositions, I had lost all heart for the fight. My only reaction was I don't want to work for, near, or with these people ever again. I told the lawyers to settle out of court as quickly as possible, get me back my contract and some kind of letter of apology, and be done with it.

It broke me. And the thing that broke me was not the hustlers and the hondlers, and it wasn't the hard, mean way of doing business. It was that I had thought there was some ground where it was safe to tell the truth, to be afraid and say, "I don't know," and there wasn't. I doubted myself and was looking for help, and you don't get to do that. There's no place for that. If you don't know, tell the bastards you do.

I was a piece of meat. Not one person one time had asked, "Wait a minute, what about her?" Not an agent, not a manager, not any of those people at the studio who were forever putting their arms around me and saying oh honey this and oh honey that. I didn't buy any of that shit, but I assumed there had to be some ethics somewhere. I assumed somebody would at least ask a question. But there was no attitude about me at all, only consternation that I would even burble out an objection. I was out of order the moment I said, "Hey, wait a minute."

I surrendered. I gave up and quit. I married a movie star and went to live in Beverly Hills and didn't work again for over six years.

I threw it all away because I was young and neurotic and hurt. I was a virgin who had the misfortune of getting raped. I'm sure there are ways that kind of head-on conflict can be avoided. Perhaps I could have finessed the situation and dealt with it better. But I didn't know how. I dealt with it the only way I could, and they won. I got into that arena, and I couldn't cut it. It was, "You lose, lady. Cash in your chips and go home." And it wasn't even anything personal.

Once again I was a failure, a quitter who couldn't take it. Other people have withstood much more. They didn't retire. They didn't run away and say, "I surrender; just leave me alone." I did. And maybe I have to work that one out for the rest of my life. During the years when a career is made, grounded, and solidified, when as an artist all your important growth takes place, I was out of the ballpark. I was sitting on my ass in Beverly Hills giving dinner parties as a movie star's wife and, when he was on location, sneaking off and doing myself brain damage with all my freak friends.

I was twenty-three years old. I'm nearly thirty-eight now, and it still gets to me. And I find that shocking. I thought I had forgotten the absolute contempt they have for your life, but the rage and the pain are still there. My God, is that nuts, when they are all dead or disabled or in somebody's pocket? Was I in some war? Am I in some war? Is my life about proving some point? I don't want to think so. But why haven't I mellowed past it? Why does it still get me? What is the quick of it, the inherent component in that situation that still hurts so much?

It is the assumption that they can defeat your dignity and take your pride away from you. And that assumption is right. They can. I guess that's the sense of betrayal I will take to my grave and possibly beyond.

My mother taught me that the world can take your

money and your job and your friends and your house and your car, and that the only things you have any control over are your honor and your pride. And the two things are really part of one thing. Honor is the only thing deserving of pride, and as long as you have your honor you have your pride. That's what Mama said.

But she was wrong.

Life is not that simple.

If you want to play in the big ballparks, your pride will be the first thing they go for. Anywhere in the world, the profiteers operate on a very accurate assumption, and that is if they can get your pride, if they can buy it or steal it, then you are theirs. They own you. And if you don't want to sell them your pride and you won't give it away either, that's okay with them, but you don't get to play.

I read over these pages and they sound to me quite like the paranoid ravings of someone trying to justify why she didn't get what she wanted. They may well be that. But I do believe that maybe that's what trying to be an artist is all about. In all the books I've read and the stories I've heard about artists, there always seems to be a lifelong struggle to keep one's pride intact. But it's made so attractive and reasonable to get rid of it that it seems like the only sane, mature, intelligent thing to do.

Get rid of that pride.

It only gets in your way.

Play ball.

Play ball and be busy again.

Hollywood, 1964

3

His opening line the first time we met was, "Well, she might clean up all right." They were working on me in the makeup room at Paramount, getting me ready to test for *Carpetbaggers,* when George Peppard ambled in and saw me sitting there with a pound of cold cream on my face and my hair up in curlers. I slumped down in my chair, and he broke up. I was sure I'd blown it.

I was already a big fan. When I saw him in *Home From the Hill,* my heart, like every other American girl's, had thumped just a little bit faster. George Hamilton and a lot of other men were in that movie, but I never noticed them.

George Peppard looked like some kind of Nordic god—six feet tall with beautiful blond hair, blue eyes, and a body out of every high school cheerleader's teenage lust fantasy. I couldn't wait to meet him when I flew out to Hollywood. That prospect was far more interesting than the movie itself.

To my great surprise, he kept coming around the whole time I was testing. He hung out with me during the breaks and called me up at night with advice about the test and how to act in front of a camera. Right from the beginning he was Mr. Take Charge: "Listen to me. I'll tell you what to do." He was thirteen years older than I and seemed like a grownup, a real adult man.

I had come in from New York in my dirty jeans and Salvation Army trenchcoat and with all the standard vehemence and prejudices of a second-year acting student.

"Fuck you, Hollywood! I'm not just another dumb star-lette!" I would open my face, and out of it would fall hours of clichés of the very young person who knows nothing at all and can only express herself with other people's hand-me-down attitudes. George would listen for a while with the kind of smile on his face that said he had heard that tape a hundred times before. Then he'd jump in and bust me for my ignorance with some kind of put-down joke that would get me laughing past my rage. I loved it.

He was as smart and funny as he was beautiful. And to have somebody like that on my case telling me what to do was like manna from heaven. George was a New York stage actor originally and understood a lot of my confusion and fear.

I was crazy about him. It was obvious that he liked me too. He wasn't spending all that time with me just because he had approval over who played the part. But he never came on to me, which only made him all the more interesting.

When the test was over, I flew back to New York to wait for word on whether or not I scored the role. I was still more or less married to Jimmy Farentino. My first night back we had another of our rows, which ended with him throwing his stuff into a suitcase and stomping out of the apartment.

It didn't have anything to do with George. We were always moving in and out, throwing each other, the furniture, and everything else out the windows and down the stairs, carrying on with all the high drama young actors love. It was lots of fun, but essentially a phase one passes through, like adolescence.

Jimmy was a ripe, raving rounder, a charming Italian

devil off the streets of Brooklyn who was working as a bartender and going to acting classes when we first got together. He used to say that where he came from you had only one of two choices. Either you went to work for the Mafia or you tried to get into show business.

We decided to get married when his Catholic background leapt up and grabbed him by the throat. He had gotten a small part as one of the beachboys in *Night of the Iguana,* the Tennessee Williams play, and one night after the show we were getting drunk at Harold's Show Spot when he turned to me and said, "Listen, you can't have me for my body alone. There's got to be more to this relationship than that." I always thought that was the girl's line, and I cracked up.

But he was serious. It was either marry him or lose his body. Shelley Winters, who was also in the play, was drinking with us and she said, "Honey, every girl ought to be married to an Italian once." She didn't really have to encourage me. Any woman who wouldn't have opted for Farentino's body would have had something the matter with her brain.

The next week after the show Shelley Winters threw us a wedding at Danny's Hideaway, an East Side saloon, and Jimmy moved into my apartment in Hell's Kitchen. Half the time he would be around, half the time he wouldn't. We were like early hippies, and it was hardly what you would call an institutionalized marriage. We certainly weren't getting on the lay-away plan at Macy's. Then *Iguana* closed and Jimmy had to go back to tending bar while I won a Tony Award for *Take Her, She's Mine.* That didn't make the marriage any easier for either of us.

I got the part in *Carpetbaggers,* and when I flew back out to California, George was waiting for me at the airport like the Prince on the White Horse. This time he did come on to me, and he was met with absolutely no resistance on any front. It was the most romantic summer of my life.

We moved into a little house on top of a hill overlooking Benedict Canyon. It was a beautiful little place in the middle of the woods, a perfect hideaway complete with raccoons and a fox and a tiny pool. I had gotten used to cold-water, six-flight walkups in New York and never realized it was possible to live like that.

Neither of us was supposed to be there. George was separated from his wife and temporarily living in an apartment until the divorce was settled. I also had to keep an address of my own, but the only time I went there was to pick up my mail. We worked on *Carpetbaggers* together during the day, then drove back to the house at night. I'd cook dinner for the two of us. We would hold hands and talk, then go to bed and make love.

I was in Hollywood in my First Movie and having a beautiful affair with a Movie Star. I thought I'd died and gone to heaven.

All my childhood fantasies about myself as a Wicked Adventuress seemed to be coming true. Even though each of us was separated, the gossip columns were full of stories about how we were both married and carrying on with each other. I was in the middle of a scandal, which was exactly where I always wanted to be.

One day when I was leaving the sound stage some gossip writer grabbed me and asked, "What exactly is your relationship with George Peppard?" I looked at him and said, "Well, we're not just good friends." Two weeks later the line was on the cover of all the movie magazines. It was one of the first times I realized the kind of trouble my mouth could get me into, but I didn't care.

The more time I spent with George the more I came

to appreciate that he wasn't just blond hair and blue eyes. A lot of movie stars are only that. They love giving the interviews. They love hair, makeup, and wardrobe. They love the parties, the houses, and the cars. They love the availability of people to sleep with. Showing up on the set and doing the work is the price they have to pay to get all that. But George was the exact opposite. What George liked was the work. He was never ever late on the set, and he had nothing but scorn for actors who weren't professional enough to keep that together.

When I showed up once about twenty minutes late because I was having trouble with my hair, George let me have it in front of everybody.

"Oh, the New York actress has finally deigned to honor us with her presence, ladies and gentlemen."

It was terribly embarrassing, but of course he was absolutely right. As furious as it made me, he was really doing me a favor. Somebody had to tell me, and it was a lot easier to take it from him than from anyone else. I was never late again. George was a consummate professional, and I learned more about that from him than I realized at the time.

George loathed the getting-your-picture-taken and giving-the-interview part of the business, but he understood they came with the job, so he tried to do them well.

One afternoon three journalists were waiting for us during the lunch break.

I said, "Oh, let 'em blow it out their ass. I'm not talking to them."

George sat me down and explained why that was wrong.

"You have to talk to them. You have to give some interviews. Don't be so hostile and smart ass. Press people have a job to do. Co-operate with them a little bit, give them what they need to do their job, and they'll give you a fair shake. Make it hard for them and they'll have the final word because they have the print."

Rather than be a little bit professional and adult about it, I was always ready to take the immediate get-off of giving somebody lip, and George stayed constantly on my case about that.

Not that he ever compromised or copped out. On the contrary. That's the thing that impressed me most. George was an intelligent, really fine actor and was determined not to lose those roots even on a straight commercial movie like *Carpetbaggers*. All through production he was continually working on the scenes and the script, trying to find ways to make them better than they were. And he found them. He had wonderful ideas about concept, performance, and scenes.

George never was one of those actors who believes his job is to take the money, hit the mark and say the lines, and let it go at that. He felt that as an above-the-title star he had the responsibility to use his muscle and power to try and make it better, and that has never stopped in him. He was unrelenting about it, to the point where a lot of executives and directors came to feel he was a pain in the ass. But the really talented people loved working with him because of all his wonderful creative energy.

George was smart and he was talented and he was inspiring. And for all the solemn, *macho* hero roles he always played, he was also funny. He had a sense of whimsy, a sense of the absurd, and when his imagination took off and he got to the child part of himself, he would giggle and carry on like a kid. He could even be funny about how straight and conservative he was.

I was impossibly arrogant and self-conscious about being hip, the way young people of my generation were. George was the first truly straight person I could communicate with.

63

Culturally, I suppose we were each other's enemies. George believed in working within the system and supporting it. I thought the system was shit and ought to be torn down, blown up, or burned. George supported the Republicans, the more right wing the better. I was for Castro and Malcolm X and anyone else who wanted to turn things around. Lenny Bruce and Che Guevara were my heroes. George liked to drink. I liked to smoke grass. He enjoyed formal sit-down dinners. I much preferred to hang out. I listened to rock 'n' roll. He listened to *Hello, Dolly!*

We seemed to have no common ground other than the fact we were in love with each other. I guess that was enough. I know I would have considered his politics and tastes totally unacceptable in anyone else. But then I doubt if one is ever gotten into a passion by someone's politics and tastes. I've loved people for them, but that's never been enough to whip me into a frenzy. Many times I've wished it was.

George was always on me for what I believed and what I liked and how I was.

He'd say, "For God's sake, will you stop smoking that crap? I don't ever want to see it around the house. And don't you ever let anybody find out about it either. You're a target now and have to live more carefully."

I found that kind of amusing. All it meant to me was that when I wanted a joint I had to go into the bathroom with a can of air spray.

Then he would jump on me about my political attitudes.

I loved to tell people how I'd been arrested along with everyone else in Greenwich Village for marching against the cops when they stopped the kids from playing their guitars in Washington Square on Sundays and closed up the coffee houses because the owners wouldn't pay them off. I wasn't that long out of acting school and hadn't forgotten that most of my teachers had been blacklisted. Just the way Americans went up to Germans after the Second World War and asked them where they had been in 1939, I would confront people at Hollywood parties and demand to know, "Where were *you* in 1959?"

We had our disagreements about all of that, but we were also having a love affair. I didn't change my principles. I just stopped talking about them around him. Of course, that's where the first drop of poison in the well goes down, but who knew?

And in some curious way, I think a lot of the things George put me down for were the very things he liked best about me. Why else would he have picked someone who, if you outlined her on a piece of paper, would add up to everything he said he hated in a woman? George liked to kid me for the way I worshiped people like Allen Ginsberg and Jack Kerouac, but when he went on to do the movie of *The Subterraneans* he truly understood the alienation Kerouac was talking about in that book. He was a loner, and so was I. Maybe it was the loner parts of ourselves that came together.

Like me, George had been an only child, but his parents were well into their forties by the time he was born. His mother had five miscarriages before she was finally able to deliver. Both his parents were the youngest children in large families, so there were lots of aunts and uncles around when he was a kid. But they were all already old, and as soon as he'd get attached to any of them, they would die.

His father had made a lot of money as a contractor, and George was brought up nicely in an upper-middle-class Middle Western way. Then the depression hit, and the family lost everything. His father had to take out his tool kit and go door to door asking for odd jobs to feed his family. It wasn't enough, so he had to leave home and move around the Midwest looking for work. George stayed in Detroit with his mother, who tried to bring in some money by giving singing lessons.

By the time he finished high school, the depression had ended and his father was able to go back to the construction business. It seemed as if everything was going to be all right again, and George enrolled in Purdue. Then just as his father had the foundations dug and the cement poured for thirty houses, he suddenly died. There was no insurance. George had to drop out of college, get a loan from the bank, and finish building all those houses himself. When he was done, he gave the money to his mother and enlisted in the Marine Corps.

After he got out, he went to Carnegie Tech on the GI Bill to study drama, then came to New York and became a member of the Actors Studio. But he didn't make it right away as an actor. He had gotten married while he was in college, and he had to spend a lot of years in cold-water flats with a wife and two kids, scuffling for work without much luck.

George didn't have it as easy as I did. For a long time it was bleak, grim, and unhappy, and he felt very much a failure. Finally, he scored in a play called *The Pleasure of His Company,* and from there went to California and got into the movies, where he became hot and famous and rich. But he never forgot how hard and miserable it had been. Maybe that's why he was so patriotic and conservative. Like so many other self-made men, he was thankful to America for allowing him his success and felt obligated to support everything else about it.

After we finished shooting *Carpetbaggers,* it was time to pack my suitcase and head back to New York to start rehearsing *Barefoot in the Park*. George had just about settled his divorce by then and was beginning to talk about getting married. But there were certain conditions. During the months we lived together he made it perfectly evident he thought actresses were all unstable, neurotic, fucked-up women, and he wasn't about to marry one, no matter how much he loved her. The deal was that I give it up, turn in my SAG card, eyelashes, and tap shoes and settle down to become a proper wife and mother, the way Nature intended.

I didn't want to give it up.

Being an actress was the only thing I'd ever done that made me feel the least bit like a competent human being who deserved a place on the planet. Over the past year I had done *Take Her, She's Mine* and *Carpetbaggers*, and now I was about to go back to Broadway in a play Neil Simon had written for me. Not that I was so terrific, but I was hot and I hoped I would start to get better.

Besides, I wasn't all that sure about getting married again. My marriage to Farentino was fun while it lasted, but it never made a whole lot of sense and we shortly went our separate ways. Why would it be any different with George? Yes, he was a lot different than Jimmy—older, wiser, more sure of himself. But I was still the same.

I kept thinking about what my mother always told me while I was growing up. She'd say, "Any stupid little nit that works in the ten-cent store can get married. It doesn't take any brains to get married. It takes brains to stay single. My God, girl, get yourself an education. Be independent so you can have some choices in your life."

But I didn't want to lose George either. I loved him too much to let him go. And maybe he was right about actresses.

I needed some time to figure it all out.

We agreed I would go do my play in New York and

he would fly in to see me as often as he could, maybe once every couple of weeks. We would keep talking and see what happened.

He wasn't at all happy about it. He thought I was sitting on the fence, and I was. But he agreed to hang in with me.

When he flew in for the opening of *Barefoot*, it turned out to be an absolute nightmare. He had reached the point where he hated everything about my being an actress, and at the party at Sardi's afterward he got very drunk. Every time someone wanted to take my picture, he grabbed another drink off the tray. When the reviews came in and we knew the show was a hit, it only made it worse.

The next day we were taken to lunch at "21" to celebrate my being the hottest little piece of ass in show business for that five minutes. I was so stoned and miserable and spaced out I didn't even know where I was.

Years later, Freddy de Cordova, the producer of the *Tonight Show*, told me he'd been there that afternoon with Mary Livingston, Jack Benny's wife, and some other high rollers in the hierarchy of the business, and when they came over to the table to congratulate me I was vulgar and rude and mean. He said they were shocked. They had never seen anyone behave so badly. And after that, needless to say, he had never been much of a fan of mine. All I could say to him was, "Freddy, I can't even remember it. It's a total blank. But I know it's true."

The next time George came in, he took me to a party at Albert Finney's house. They had done a picture together and become friends. George liked him a lot and so did I, and the three of us took to meeting for drinks after the show. When George had to go back to California, he told Finney, "Well, keep an eye on my girl, will you?"

Finney was in New York touring with *Luther*. When

he left England he announced he was planning to screw his way around the world. Every female in New York between fourteen and sixty was calling him on the phone, just begging to go to bed with him. I was probably the only actress in town who didn't have that in mind. I have always been pretty much of a one-man-at-a-time woman, and I was already in love with George. But I found Finney inspiring and exciting. I was very much in awe of him. We were almost the same age, and he was already a great, great actor. He was everything I wanted to be but wasn't.

I started hanging out at Finney's house during the afternoons I didn't have a matinee, spending hours with him listening to him talk about acting. There were always other performers around, people like Tom Courtenay and some of the other Brits working in New York. Sometimes after our shows we would all get together for drinks at Downey's. I was just one of the guys.

And then of course the inevitable happened. I fell in love with him. There is never anything more seductive than forbidden fruit. The one person you are not supposed to have is the one person you are going to want. I knew it was only a fantasy that couldn't come to anything. Finney made it absolutely clear he wasn't in love with me. But it didn't seem to make any difference.

For the first time in my life I was in love with two men at the same time. George was offering to take care of me, to solve my life and make it simple and good. But he wanted me to stop being an actress. Finney was offering me nothing at all except some of his time and body. But he didn't want me to stop being an actress. What I wanted was both things in one man. But you don't get that. It doesn't come that way. So I was being pulled in both directions at once. It's possible that had something to do with my falling apart and ending up in Payne Whitney.

I came out of the hospital a cynical, angry, frightened person and went back to the play with a very different set of priorities. I was no longer so concerned about getting Bob Redford's approval. I stopped worrying about how to do it better. My only responsibility was to show up. It didn't matter if I was any good or not. Nobody seemed to care about that. All they wanted was my physical presence. As long as they had that, my personal problems couldn't have mattered less to them.

And they weren't wrong. Not at all. One of the first big lessons you have to learn is that whatever personal *angst* you may have comes second. And if your personal *angst* gets between you and the gig, then you don't have any right to be doing the gig.

The rules are simple: If you've got problems, go to an analyst. During the day. On your own time. And that's what I started to do. Four times a week I would trot over to the analyst's office and plop myself down on the couch for an hour, just the way I was supposed to. Then I'd go to the theater and get to work so I would have the money to pay him.

By the time I returned to *Barefoot in the Park*, Albert Finney had left town with his play and disappeared from my life. George never found out about him, and I never told him. He continued to work around his shooting schedule to be with me as much as he could, doing everything possible to make sure I was all right. He seemed to be the only person in the world who gave a damn whether I was dead or alive, other than those who worried whether I would show up at the theater.

I was still in *Barefoot* when George's mother suddenly died. When he called to tell me, I could hear in his voice how pained and distraught he was. I wanted to be with him, to help him the way he helped me, but I had to do the show. The only thing I could think to say was what I'd heard as a kid when something terrible like that happened. My mother always took a tough line about those things, and in the arrogance of my youth that's what I gave to George.

"Oh, man, I'm really sorry about it. But, look, everybody dies. Weeping and moaning won't bring her back. You never liked her much anyway. You're going to have to get past it."

Not a very sensitive response.

After the funeral, George called again and said he was flying to Europe to be by himself for a while. He had a lot of things to think about. He'd write me soon.

Every morning I ran down to the mailbox hoping his letter would be there. For weeks it wasn't, and then one day it was. I sat down on the stairs and tore it open. He said it was all over. He couldn't get past how callous I had been and didn't want to be with me any more. I think I was too dazed to cry.

Finally I climbed back up to my apartment and tried to reach him on the telephone. It took hours to find him, but when at last I got through it didn't change anything. He was through with me. And that made a terrible kind of sense. He was the one person who cared about me, and I'd blown it by being neurotic and emotionally unreliable. I got what was coming to me. It seemed like the final failure.

I started hitting the streets with a passion.

Instead of trying to improve myself and be a better person and a better actress, I began running with my good and true low-life buddies who didn't give a shit if I was neurotic or not. Everybody was crazy. Crazy was your currency. It wasn't something you tried not to be. It was something you were proud of and worked hard to embellish. After the show, instead of trying to hang out with the uptown grownups, I would head right back to my apartment, which would be full of people who were as lost, crazy, disillusioned, and pained as I was.

I smoked a lot of dope. I made it with a lot of guys. I tried every way I could think of to act just as bad and outrageously as I could. If I was invited to a party uptown, I would go, but I would make a great point of not putting on a dress. I'd wear my fatigues, and I'd be sure to take two or three of my buddies with me, who much of the time were in no condition to be let out of their cages much less turned loose on polite society.

Of course, there was vengeance in it, childish, self-destructive vengeance. All the grownups had been telling me I was a Bad Girl, and I was saying, "You think that's a Bad Girl? Hell, I'll show you what a Bad Girl is! . . . But I show up for the play. I'm not crazy. See? See me be there? I'm there. And that's all I'm gonna do." I was in a rage because somewhere in my head it seemed to me I had begged for help and all I had gotten was a good strong read-out on the rules. And if you break the rules you don't get help. You get punishment.

Stanley Kramer got me out of *Barefoot* to make *Ship of Fools* for him. The deal was I would leave the play for fifteen weeks over the summer and then when I finished the film come back to the play for fifteen weeks beyond the run of my contract. I was delighted. I wanted out so badly it didn't matter what the movie was. I didn't even have to read the script.

George was back in California when I got out there, and we slowly and cautiously started to come together again. By now my ears were not nearly so jaded about being an actress. It looked pretty fucked to me from where I sat. To the extent I was capable of a plan, it was to do *Ship of Fools*, finish up *Barefoot,* then take some time off to try to figure out whether or not to go on.

By the time shooting was completed on *Ship of Fools*, George was getting ready to leave for London where he would spend the year making more movies. He asked me to come with him. I said I would try. He was still the only person in my life saying, "I want to take care of you."

My manager called Saint-Subber, the producer of *Barefoot*, to find out what it would take to get me out of my contract. The play was already sold out for the next year, but Saint-Subber still wanted thirty-five thousand dollars. That was ten grand more than Richard Burton had to pay the producers of *Camelot* when he wanted to get out for a little movie called *Cleopatra*. I didn't have anything like that in the bank, so we called Joe Levine, who had produced *Carpetbaggers* independently for Paramount.

When I turned out to be the big buzz in the movie, Levine kicked himself for not having made a deal with me before I had gotten hot. He was always after me to do more pictures with him. He would call and say, "Want an Oscar? I'll get you an Oscar. I got one for Sophia. I'll get one for you."

A lot of producers wanted me to do pictures and would have gladly bought me out of *Barefoot* to go to work for them. But what I wanted was to not go to work. At least not right away. The way we presented it to Levine was that the thirty-five thousand would be applied against a picture I would owe him, but I wouldn't have to start for another six months to a year.

He said, "Okay. You got it."

We said, swell, but we have to have it fast, within the next two weeks. Otherwise, if I didn't go back to *Barefoot*, Saint-Subber would sue me.

Levine said, "No problem. You'll have the check tomorrow."

I breathed a huge sigh of relief and told George to save me a seat; I'd be flying to London with him.

But the check didn't come the next day. Nor did it come the day after that or the day after that. We tried calling Levine on the phone, but he was never there and he never called back. The time was getting shorter and shorter, and I was starting to go crazy from the pressure.

Finally, we did some snooping and found out we weren't ever going to get Joe Levine on the phone. He'd gone broke. All the millions he had made on *Carpetbaggers* had been lost on other pictures. Sometimes life gets tough for the moguls.

I cursed Joe Levine to the heavens for not having the decency to tell me, for messing with my life like that. I was hysterical, out of control, and exhausted. Everything was coming down on me, and I didn't know what to do.

Then I thought of Marty Rackin at Paramount. Not that he had any reason to help me. He had every reason to do the opposite. I already owed him some movies, and it would be totally against his self-interest to make it possible for me to put off my commitments. But he listened to me, then said, "Well, kid, I'll try to come up with something. Maybe we can work the money off of your Paramount contract." Twenty-four hours later the check was in my hands. I think he saved my life.

To quote Dory Previn, "The dealer winks and the game gets rougher."

When I got to London with George all I wanted to do was vegetate. Truffaut called about *Fahrenheit 451,* and I couldn't even take the meeting. The Mirisches asked me to meet with them about *Hawaii.* Woody Allen wanted to see me for *What's New, Pussycat?* I didn't show up for them either. Nothing made any sense. I didn't know who I was. I didn't know what I was doing in London. George and I were entering into heavy duty psychic warfare.

The relationship had become torturous for both of

74

us. But I suppose it was what we both needed, so we were trying to work it out. When it got too bad, I would pack my suitcase and go off to Europe, where I would bum around and stay so loaded I wouldn't even know what country I was in. Then, when I could get myself together, I would come back to London and live with him in his townhouse until I had to go off again. That's how the whole year went. I felt like a creep. George was paying all the bills. I had never lived off a man before.

At the end of the year George had to come back to California to start *The Third Day* for Warner Brothers. Warners wanted me to be in it with him and offered me a hundred thousand dollars. I said I'd do it. Everyone but George had told me what a good move it would be. I had been off the screen for a year and wasn't quite so hot any more. Even if the script wasn't terrific, George and I could make it work, just as we had in *Carpetbaggers*. George wasn't all that happy about it. I was still on the fence, still hanging on. I still had dreams of being a star.

The move turned out not quite as good as everyone thought it would be. I could tell while I was making the picture that it was going to be just another piece of garbage. And I knew I was terrible. I couldn't even be good in garbage.

One day toward the end of the shooting, George showed up with a big diamond ring and said, "Come on, Elizabeth. Enough of this. Let's get engaged."

I said okay and took it.

I asked him could we please hold off on the wedding date for a while. I had read the script of *Cross My Heart and Hope to Die* and wanted to give it one more try. As I saw it, it was my last chance to be a real actress.

That little fantasy came to an end when I was dumped from the picture after *Ship of Fools* was screened. Suddenly the telephone stopped ringing. Suddenly no one was around any more. I didn't even get a call from my agent. The only person I could get on the phone was George.

That's how you know when you are frozen out. Unlike the theater, which, for all its bullshit, at least has one undeniable moment of truth when the curtain goes up, the movies never have any kind of definitive direct confrontation. Everyone keeps right on smiling "Hello, sweetie" whenever they see you, only they make a point of staying out of your way so they *don't* see you.

I was all over. Washed up. Nobody wanted me.

In a way it solved my problem by pulling me off the fence I'd been sitting on for a year. I could no longer think of myself as an actress because I could no longer get a job acting. It was as simple and neat as that.

I suppose I should have felt some relief, but all I felt was failure. Once again I'd blown it. That was the first thought that invaded my head when I woke up in the morning, and it squatted there reproaching me until I went to sleep at night. I couldn't make it as an actress. I couldn't make it as a crazy. The only choice left was to get married and try to make it as a wife.

I told George, "Okay, I'm ready if you are. Let's do it."

I know now that what I needed was someone who believed in me, someone who would say, "Yes, you can do it. Of course you can do it, and this is what you're going to do. I'm going to make you do it." But the only solace available was from George, and he was saying the direct opposite of that. And it didn't sound wrong.

He would tell me, "You are not a failure as a human being and you are not a failure as a woman. You are only a failure as an actress. Don't you see?"

I saw.

How much easier it is to think, "Yes, I failed because I am a better, finer, more sensitive person, not because I couldn't cut it." Why, it takes the edge right off it.

We started planning the wedding.

4

After we were married I busied myself with being a professional wife. George said to me, "All that creativity and energy and caring you put into your work I want you to put into me." That sounded fine. I didn't have any place else to put them.

George wanted a home for his two children by his first wife, so I spent months hunting for a house. I finally found one, a marvelous country ranch house on a cul-de-sac overlooking Coldwater Canyon. It had a huge barn-like living room, pitched and beamed with a lot of wood, and an enormous stone fireplace. There was a wonderful loft out over the fireplace and a den and a breakfast room and a dining room and four bedrooms, about fourteen rooms in all plus a little outside guest house next to the pool that would make George a perfect office. When you walked to the end of the property there was a magnificent view down into the canyon. I loved it. It was a comfortable, warm, pretty place. When I took George to see it he loved it too. I got myself a decorator's card and started hunting for antiques and fabrics.

George had assured me, "There may be a time in your life when you'll want to do a little show or something, here or there, and that will be okay." The point was I was to turn in my professional status, which was easy enough to do since I couldn't get a job anyway.

It was put to the test a couple of months after we married and moved into the new house.

We were getting ready to take off on a camping trip with his kids. George had been making one film after another after another, just killing himself with work. Finally, he was able to put two weeks aside to do nothing but relax.

The day before we were to leave, I got a call from my agent.

"Elizabeth, what would you think about doing the movie of *Barefoot in the Park*?"

I was stunned.

Hal Wallis had bought the film rights to the play for Paramount right after it opened, and for two years the question of Who Would Play the Part had been an ongoing topic of conversation in the business. At first everyone assumed it would either be some big movie star like Natalie Wood or else me. But then I became smelly fish, and if I was remembered at all it was for having been difficult in some forgotten snarl at Paramount. Besides, Hal Wallis had already gone on record as saying, "I'm not an Ashley fan. I didn't like her work in the play." I was told he had never seen me in the play, but it didn't really matter. I was the very last choice.

My agent told me all of this had now changed. According to him, there had just been another shakeup in the board of directors at Paramount. Charles Bludhorn and the Gulf and Western people, now running the company from New York, were curious about the delay on the picture. Wallis was having trouble getting it cast. Bludhorn said "Well, what about the girl who did the play?" When he was told what had gone down between me and Paramount, he supposedly answered, "Somebody must ask her nicely."

There was also a political aspect to it. Wallis had been one of those producers who pretty much ran his own show at Paramount. The Gulf and Western crowd wanted to put an end to that sort of thing. Little by little they were trying to scale down his power.

To placate Wallis, they decided to test a number of known actresses for the part and make the final decision on the basis of what the film looked like. The tests were all going to be directed by Blake Edwards, who was too busy with other projects to direct the picture itself. My agent explained that although I would have to test, there was an understanding that I would probably get it. I was the one Bludhorn wanted. Could I read the script immediately? He'd have a messenger bring it right over.

I hung up the phone, went to the living room and told George what had happened. He was down on the floor rolling up the backpacks for the next day. He tried not to say anything that would put any pressure on me, but I could see how disappointed he was. It meant I couldn't go on the camping trip. Much more seriously, it meant I still hadn't really committed myself to not being an actress. I hoped the script would be terrible.

The messenger rang the doorbell. I took the script into the bedroom, sat down on the bed, and started reading. It was wonderful, the best possible adaptation of the play.

All I felt was strung out. Once again there was the terrible pressure of being pulled in two different directions at the same time. No matter which way I went I would be making a mistake and not doing what I was supposed to do. If I turned it down, no one would take me seriously enough to offer me another film. If I took it, I'd be in that vise of living with a man and doing something he hated.

I reached for the phone and called my agent.

I said, "Herman, the script is terrific, but I'm not going to do the test."

There was silence at the other end. I went on.

"Herman, I realize that as an agent you cannot possibly be in that position, so what I'm going to do is retire. This makes it official. Don't send me scripts. Don't call me about work. Take my name off the list. It's all over."

I went back into the living room and told George what I had decided. He was gratified and relieved. The next day before we left he disappeared for an hour and came back with a diamond necklace. Jane Fonda did the movie of *Barefoot in the Park*, and I didn't work again for six years.

I threw myself into doing what I was supposed to do.

I hired and ran a staff.

I organized the chauffeuring of George's children to and from school.

I did the work charts for the houseman, the servants, and George's secretary.

I became a hostess, giving sit-down dinner parties for anywhere from twelve or fourteen people to as many as a hundred. George liked a formal, rather baronial style of life where all the social events were mapped out in advance. Each Friday evening I would sit down with him and show him the plan for the following week: what we would be doing, who the guests were, what would be served.

I could do all that and do it pretty well. I may have grown up poor, but I knew what Irish linen cutwork tablecloths and napkins were from visiting my Great-aunt Rena's house in Augusta, Georgia. I even got a reputation for giving warm, elegant parties.

I understood that when people are working in pictures they have been up since five or six o'clock in the morning, and you can't make them wait until nine or nine-thirty to eat dinner. Forget chic. At my dinner parties they were served at eight. And I understood the only way to keep them from getting so drunk they lost their appetites was to have wine rather than hard liquor waiting for them when they came in, along with plenty of really good hors d'oeuvres.

I found something like thirty cases of a 1934 Chateau Palmer at an estate auction, and I would always put an open bottle on every table. As soon as guests walked in, they could sit down next to whomever they wanted to talk to, pour themselves a glass of wine, eat some hors d'oeuvres and get relaxed and comfortable.

My parties were imaginative and pretty, and it wasn't hired pretty. When we decided to have a tent party at Thanksgiving for two hundred people, I didn't have to rely on Abbey Rents. I found a transparent tent and got a couple of my gypsy buddies to put it up four days early. Then we decorated it ourselves with all sorts of beautiful fresh vegetables. We strung the vegetables together and hung them up with wonderful ribbon checked and striped in autumn colors. I tied up all the bows myself. We carved out about fifty pumpkins, filled them with more fresh vegetables, and put one on each table as a centerpiece. People took them home, so nothing was wasted. I flew in black market baby lobsters from Maine and oysters from New Orleans. We had a real New Orleans seafood bar, where our cook, Earl, cracked those oysters and served them up right in front of everyone.

And my guest lists were never predictable. At my house, young filmmakers like Lazlo Kovaks and Bill Fraker got to meet veterans like George Stevens, Sr. Gregory Peck got to hang out with rock-and-rollers. People didn't dread coming. They had a good time and always came back.

I think I did that very well. A lot of those Beverly Hills women could make that way of life into a full-time career. I tried to be like them.

It wasn't good enough.

It was exactly the same pressure as acting but without any of the rewards. The pressure was to have it the way George needed it and wanted it, and I could never seem to do that. I could never please him.

His work was keeping him in a constant state of exhaustion and frustration, and when actors are under that sort of tension they get nasty and they get mean. They don't have the energy left over to be nice or fun. I know that now from my own life, but I didn't know it then.

George would come home from the studio wasted and angry, then take it all out on me because he didn't like what I served him for dinner.

"I am working twelve hours a day. I am exhausted. When I come home I want it pleasant and I want good food cooked the way I like it. Why can't I have that? I am working hard to pay these bills. Everybody around here is living off my efforts, and they're not living badly. It's not a bad life. So why can't I have it *exactly* the way I want it?"

There's no answer to that. The real issue was that he wanted me to make him happy and blamed me because I couldn't. I blamed myself just as much as he did. Why couldn't I make him happy? That was really the only thing I had to do.

I began to feel less and less effective, and more and more ludicrous.

I got myself another analyst and plugged away at it four times a week. The analyst sat there silently. If he had something to tell me, I never heard it. But I kept on going so I could feel at least I had that covered.

"Okay, God, you see it. I'm going. I'm doing my time."

What tormented George so badly was that he was caught between being an actor and being a movie star. He did not start out as an untalented pretty nothing who had to be grateful for any piece of meat that was thrown his way. He was intelligent and talented, but because he was six feet tall with blond hair and blue eyes, he had been put in the slot of being a movie star at a time when the studios were still very powerful and expected you to play the game by their rules. George was younger than people like Mitchum and Brando, but he was older than Warren Beatty, Bob Redford, and the other actors of my generation who came up in the 1960s when the old system had pretty much fallen apart and the power was up for grabs.

Not that he was ever some kind of lamb who went blithely on his way to the slaughter. When he first came to California he lived in San Diego rather than Hollywood so he could keep a distance from that world and not get trapped by it. But I don't think it was possible to be a male movie star who looked like he did and got hot when he did and not be trapped by it. George fought a lot of studios about a lot of things, but they were heavier battles than he had the power to sustain.

He used to tell me, "An actor always has to be ready to sell the farm. The only power you ever have is your willingness to go broke. The only thing they can ever take away from you is everything you've got, so if you're willing to give that up they have no power over you."

He knew all about the money trap, but he got caught in it just the same.

What George wanted was to make enough money to get out. A lot of men who are movie stars have that dream. It rarely becomes a reality. They usually destroy themselves trying to do the work that will get them the money to save themselves. And like most movie stars, George had a plan.

He bought a ranch. It would take about ten years to develop it fully, but then he would have a magnificent

85

cow-calf operation that would be mostly profit. The catch was that to get to that point he would have to clear about $700,000 in hard cash every year to pay for it.

That was the main reason he was working so hard. He had made a deal with Universal to get the money, and now had to do a lot of junk for them. What he failed to recognize was that not even he was strong enough to do that much shit without it killing him.

He started drinking. It was the only way he could cope with that mentality and do those pictures. And every time he made another drunken phone call in the middle of the night, it just shortened the quota on the number of days he had left before he too would be considered "too difficult."

I seemed to be the only one around who saw or cared about what it was taking out of him. George had plenty of advisors, but they were all much older men who always counseled him to play by the rules of the game. I tried to tell him what I saw, but it was like a voice in the wilderness. Everything I said was diametrically opposed to the advice being given by people who were getting large percentages of his salary for their "expertise."

One day when he was off at the studio I found a script he had left in the living room. It was *The Heart Is a Lonely Hunter,* an adaptation of the Carson McCullers novel. I started flipping through it and immediately got caught up. It was wonderful. I couldn't wait until he came home. As soon as he walked through the door I was on him about it.

"Oh, George, you have to do this. It's beautiful."

He shook his head.

"No, I've already turned it down."

I didn't understand.

"My God, why?"

He told me his agent said it wouldn't be good for him. He was a leading man. He couldn't play a character who was weak or possibly homosexual. It would ruin his career.

He gestured there was nothing more to say about it, but I couldn't let it go. The script was too good.

"I don't get it, George. You're hot. You've made *How the West Was Won.* You've made *Home from the Hill.* You've made *Breakfast at Tiffany's.* You've made *The Victors.* There's a lot of money riding on you. You're a big movie star. You can do whatever you want to do. You don't have to keep doing all that other shit."

I still had the ignorance and arrogance of somebody who has never been on the line, who has never been under that kind of pressure. I started using stupid phrases like "selling out" and all the other easy rhetoric that falls out of the mouths of babes. As if he hadn't been through it a hundred times before in the privacy of his own mind, I started lecturing him about Marlon Brando and how he'd been able to rebel against the system and do good work.

I saw how angry and hurt I was making him, but I couldn't stop running my mouth.

Finally, he snapped back at me, "What do you **know?** Really, Elizabeth, what the hell do you know about it? You only see it as shit if it's big and expensive. If someone does a piece of shit in some Greenwich Village basement, you think it's fine, sensitive art."

We were both right and both wrong.

I felt certain he was listening to people who were totally out of touch with anything that was going on outside of Beverly Hills, Las Vegas, Wall Street and Palm Springs. But on the other hand, what did *I* know? I certainly hadn't handled my own career with much skill.

"Besides," he went on, "do you have any idea how

much money it takes to keep this style of life going?" He made a sweeping gesture that took in the whole house and everything in it. "Where do you think all this comes from?"

I said, "Oh, George, I don't even like this way of life. Why don't we just get rid of everything and live low rent and loose? Throw it all away. Start over again. Change your life while you still can."

He laughed a bitter, bitter laugh.

"Don't you think I'm trying to? But I have to make the goddamn *money* before I can change my life! Is that so hard to understand?"

Like a dog after a bone, I couldn't let go.

"George, I think all those people who are telling you what to do are fucked! I do not think they have your best interests at heart. I think they are fucking you over! I think they are lying to you, and I think they are cheating you!"

He glowered at me and cursed.

"God damn you! Why do you undercut everything I try to do? I need solace. I need affection. I need understanding. But most of all I need support. And all you do is shoot down my friends and undercut my advisors and the people I depend on!"

He was right.

I shut up.

I got very, very silent.

The deeply silent years had begun.

And I watched the man I loved, one of the finest people I'd ever known, slowly shredded by the so-called wisdom of the so-called wise men in the business. And I watched what happened when he tried to run counter to that and fight it. I saw how if they don't get you coming, they get you going. I saw the hypocrisy. I saw the lies. I saw the ugliness.

And I saw how people like George are treated with silent contempt because all they want is for the actor to show up and do what he did yesterday. They don't want to know what he thinks. They don't want his ideas. They don't want it done better. George never stopped asking, "Why does it have to be shitty? Why can't it be good?" And they would humor him when they had no intention of making it good.

They don't want it good. They want it Thursday.

And I saw what that did to him. I saw the murder of a human spirit. I saw how helpless he was, and I understood his rage. I understood why he drank so much when he came home at night. God knows I could have been more understanding, but I was the one who was there and that makes it hard. It's a lot easier to be understanding from a distance.

I saw the vortex and I saw the mandala. I saw the battles he was fighting, and I knew they were futile. I knew it was a no-win situation.

But I felt completely helpless to do anything about it.

What could I say? "Give up"?

New York, 1967

5

It started with cancer and ended with the birth of our son.

Having a kid was one of the first things George and I disagreed about. Almost immediately after we were married he said, "Okay, now we'll have a baby." My answer was, "Hey, wait a minute. I think maybe we should try to get our own lives together first." Julie and Brad, George's children by his first wife, were bright, good-looking kids, but they were still kids and problems are part of that package. I remember thinking, "Jesus, I don't know if I'm ready to deal with this."

Reluctantly, George agreed to wait.

Two years later we were in New York for a picture George was doing with George Seaton, and I went to Dr. Louis Finger for a Pap test. Louis was an old friend of George's; he'd met him through Lee Strasberg. Whenever we were in town, he was our doctor. You're supposed to have a Pap smear twice a year, and it was time. I went to him as a matter of course without thinking anything much about it.

The next day I dropped by his office to get the results. They weren't good. The test had come up positive. There was that terrible, sinking feeling in my gut, then it flashed through my head that here as last was the destiny that had been waiting for me all these years. Cancer runs in my family. My grandmother died a horrible death from it. My mother had been operated on for cancer of the uterus just the year before. Now it was my turn. It looked like cancer of the cervix.

Louis saw what I was going through and tried to take the edge off it. He held my hand and said, "Look, Elizabeth, there are about two hundred reasons why a woman can have a bad Pap. Cancer is one of them. We have to do more tests. We have to biopsy it."

He called the specialist and made me an appointment for the next day. I spent the rest of the afternoon wandering around the city, trying to come to terms with it. I always thought I'd be able to handle it if it happened, but this was the first time I really had to look it in the face.

Okay, bottom line is I may die.

Middle line, this may be the beginning of something that won't be terribly hard for a long time.

It's possible I may be all right.

(Who are you kidding?)

I summoned up every bit of will power in me to stay calm and dispassionate. But I was scared. I didn't want to die.

By the time I got back to the hotel I had made up my mind not to say anything to George until I had the biopsy and knew for sure. He was already too burdened by everything else in his life.

The moment he walked through the door I blurted it all out. I was too afraid not to tell him.

He was wonderful. He put everything that was bothering him out of his head and made me feel confident and strong. We ordered up a bottle of wine and a lovely dinner from room service, and by the end of the evening were laughing and joking together like we hadn't done for years.

That's one thing about George Peppard. If you need somebody to put your back up against in a riot, he's the very best. George takes care of the people he loves.

The next morning I went to the specialist for what they tell you is a simple office procedure. They give you a shot of Demerol, put you on the table, surgically remove the opening of the cervix where the bad cells are, then cauterize it to stop the bleeding.

After he finished, the doctor told me he still couldn't be sure if it was cancer or not. It was in some kind of in-between stage. I would have to wait six months for my next Pap smear and see how it looked then. Meanwhile, there was a list of all sorts of things to do and not do. The main thing not to do was make love with my husband. That had to wait another ten weeks.

I went back to see Louis the next day, and he explained why the specialist had told me that.

"The only reason not to make love is because it will almost certainly result in pregnancy. One of the reasons you haven't gotten pregnant before is because your cervix was quite closed by all the bad cells."

Now it was as wide open as the Lincoln Tunnel.

He went on to make a recommendation.

"If there's no reason not to get pregnant, I think this would be an excellent time. No one really knows why, but in many cases, if a woman has cancer in any. of the reproductive organs and becomes pregnant, the cancer will disappear. That's why they study the placenta so closely. It's one of those extraordinary, magical things about the female body."

Louis said he would be meeting with George later that afternoon. He wanted to tell us separately so we could each deal with it as we thought best.

I didn't quite know what to do with the information.

George knew exactly what to do with it.

Because of all the exhaustion and tension and separation, he jumped me more in the next few weeks than he had in the past two years. He was Jim Dandy to the

93

rescue. So in addition to giving me the most beautiful child in the world, he may also have saved my life. I've not had a questionable Pap since.

I found out I was going to have the baby while we were gearing up to move to Rome for George's next picture. I was working on my Italian and packing up what we would take with us when I began to feel peculiarly nauseous and tired. It never occurred to me I was pregnant. I was still getting my period. But when I saw the doctor he said, "No, there's nothing the matter. You're just two months pregnant."

I was amazed how elated that made me.

But he wasn't through.

"I'm afraid you'll probably lose it because you're spotting. That's why you thought you were still menstruating."

The roller coaster I was climbing for those two seconds took a sudden dive downward.

"Elizabeth, I'm going to give you these pills. Take them every six hours. Over the next few weeks you will either miscarry or you won't. You probably will. And if you do, you should. Trust nature. She has a wonderful way of not allowing a pregnancy to take if it's not supposed to."

I knew I wanted that baby more than anything. The fact that I was carrying it inside me already made me feel more like a tangible human than I ever had before.

"Well, what if I took it supereasy and tried not to jar anything? Wouldn't that help?"

He looked me straight in the eyes and said, "Yes, I suppose I could put you in bed and all that, and perhaps you would not miscarry. But I think nature knows more than we do. Go on with your life. Do everything you usually do. We'll find out soon enough."

I did what he told me, praying all the while I wouldn't lose it. Two days later the spotting was over.

George couldn't get the grin off his face for days. He bounded around the house like a teenager in heat. He had wanted that child so badly. And it meant everything to him when he saw how much I wanted it too. He had never known that before because I had never known it. I was finally able to make him happy.

George went off to Rome, and I joined him the next month, just as soon as Dr. Klein, my obstetrician, gave me the go-ahead. We moved into a huge, beautiful old villa, the same house Elizabeth Taylor lived in when she filmed *Cleopatra*. It was like a new beginning. I had felt so useless before, and now I felt wonderful. I had some purpose. There *was* something I could do.

I never felt so good or looked better. I never had any morning sickness, and for the first time in my life I was truly beautiful. Normally, I'm a rather hard-looking woman, with very angular features. The best it usually gets for me is if someone calls me "handsome" or "interesting." But I got very soft-looking, the way pregnant women do, and for the first time in my life I had real tits. Instead of maternity clothes I wore low-cut Mexican peasant blouses to show them off for all they were worth. I knew I'd never look that good again.

My anxiety demon disappeared completely. I had no worries. I was taken care of. I didn't have to work. I didn't have to do anything except be pregnant. It was the longest period in my life I have ever been at peace. It was the only thing that ever gave me peace. From the moment he was conceived, Christian brought me joy. And right from the start I had an honest-to-goodness relationship with him. Even while he was in my belly I could tell he was whimsical and imaginative and good.

The house was run by Gina and Angelo, an Italian couple from Perugia. They spoke no English and I hadn't really learned any Italian, but we communicated just fine. Gina made her own pasta, and for five months it was, *"Mangia, mangia, mangia."* They had no problem getting through to me. I ate like a pig.

We were joined for a while by Orson Welles, who was on the picture with George. The first time we met he won me over completely. His opening line was, "Dahling girl, I've always had a weakness for pregnant ladies." Five minutes later he was ranting and complaining about his hotel, and I said, "Well why not come stay with us? There's plenty of room." Without so much as a "Do you really mean it?" he was there, and that was weeks and weeks of absolute bliss. He upset everything. He went to the village for goat's milk and made us spaghetti carbonara. He drank. He told wonderful stories full of hardcore gossip about where all the bodies are buried. He took me on carriage rides around Rome with his fourteen-year-old daughter Bibi.

By the time George finished the picture I was eight months pregnant and so huge I couldn't sit head-in to the table. Before we left California Dr. Klein had told me, "I don't like my women to gain more than fifteen pounds. But then you don't have to worry about that. You never gain weight." I usually had to live on milkshakes to stay at 108.

When we got back to Los Angeles he took one look at me and freaked. "My God, woman, you weigh 145 pounds! You are going on a diet immediately!" So it was onto the carrot sticks and the celery and the cucumbers. I looked like some kind of overgrown mushroom, but I was feeling great and George was feeling great and everything seemed terrific.

The only thing I wanted to do was go to the movies

with George. The day before I gave birth we were getting ready to go to the matinee, and I had become so immense I couldn't even get on the pants with the drawstring. George was standing right behind me trying to keep my spirits up, and when I caught our reflections in the mirror I started to cry. There he was all blond, blue-eyed, and handsome, and I was this huge dumpling with stringy hair and pimples. I sobbed, "I remember when I was the pretty one!" George gave me a big hug and said, "Well, babe, you obviously so adore being pregnant, you're just so crazy about those boobs, that you're never going to let go of it." I was already a couple of weeks overdue. Everyone I knew was saying, "Come on and have that baby, will you?"

Before I went to bed that night I waddled off to the kitchen when no one was looking and, diet or no diet, devoured an entire Sara Lee chocolate cake by myself. I woke up at three in the morning in the middle of a puddle. The water had gone, and the contractions were starting. I shook George awake, and he brought in Brad and Julie, as he had promised them he would. Each time a contraction began, it made me giggle. It was like hitting a funny bone. The four of us sat there on the bed laughing together, timing the contractions with a stop watch to make sure this was really it. When it became clear that it was, we made the call to Dr. Klein. He said, "Well, mosey on down to the hospital in about an hour, and I'll see you there. It's about time."

As we got in the car, I flashed on the chocolate cake I had eaten and how Dr. Klein would find it out when they gave me the enema. All the way over to the hospital my mind was so bolluxed up that the only thing I could get a fix on was how furious he would be with me for falling off the diet. When the nurses came at me with the enema bag, I tried to talk them out of it. "No, no. That's okay. I don't need it. I already went." Dr. Klein arrived in the middle of this psychodrama. When he asked what was going on I started crying and confessed, "I ate the whole Sara Lee chocolate cake!" He said, "Elizabeth, you can have the remains of the Sara Lee chocolate cake all over the the walls of this delivery room or you can have an enema. It is simple." Even the nurses laughed.

I went into labor about five A.M. and kept waiting for the bad part to happen. It never did. I had studied all the books on natural childbirth and knew how to apply what they told me. They involved precisely the same things I already did as an actress. The Method school of acting teaches you that through concentration and breathing you can induce relaxation. Natural childbirth works the same way. By concentrating on your breathing you can relax the voluntary muscles so they won't tense up and stop the involuntary muscles that deliver the baby from doing their job. The pain of childbirth comes from those two sets of muscles working against each other.

I had one bad moment when a nurse was trying to examine me at the same time a contraction came. I blew my concentration, tightened up, and almost went through the roof. Except for that, I was completely cool. I stuffed some Kleenex in my ears, to cut off the sounds of the other women yelling so that I could relax, and continued on with my breathing exercises.

Twelve hours later I was still in labor. The baby was very large. Every time he started to come down he'd go back up again because the passage was too small for him to get through. But I had no doubt I could deliver him. I just wanted to stay there and do it, no matter how long it took. Finally Dr. Klein said, "Okay, Elizabeth, enough is enough. We're going to do a Caesarian section."

I was terrified of the knife, but begged him not to knock me out. I knew the drugs would affect the baby's brain. He gave me an epidural that kept me wide awake,

98

and when I began to tense up as I watched him go to work he said, "So okay, will you stop bitching? I've already made the incision." There was absolutely no pain. Less than three minutes later Christian came out hollering. They held him up so I could see him, then knocked me out and sewed me back up.

When I woke up in the hospital bed my first thoughts were, "Did that really happen? Did I really have a baby or did I dream it? Where's my baby?"

I heard people talking on the other side of the curtain and tried to get their attention, but I couldn't make a sound. The Caesarian had traumatized the gut muscles you need for speech. I reached over and rattled the curtain. A relative of the other woman in the room stuck his head through. When he saw I couldn't speak, he disappeared, then returned with a pencil and a pad of paper. I wrote down "baby" and "nurse."

A minute later the nurse came in with Christian and placed him right on my chest.

I had never seen a newborn baby before.

He looked like a little old man who sells rugs or a nine-pound vanilla pudding with some holes in it, but he wasn't banged up and bruised like most babies who come through the birth canal. Everyone in the room kept saying, "Oh, now this is a beautiful baby!" The nurse gave me something to put me back to sleep. As I drifted off I was thinking, "I couldn't agree more; I couldn't agree more."

Twenty-four hours later they let me nurse him for the first time. As the nurses put him to my breast they said, "Now he may not want to take the milk right away. And it's nothing to worry about if he doesn't." I remembered how my mother had told me she wasn't able to nurse me because her milk had gone. But as soon as they set him down he went for it.

And then I really knew.

I had always felt like a vaccination that didn't take. Unless I had some solid proof that I existed, I couldn't be sure.

But from that moment on I never had that doubt again.

I *knew* I was here.

I *knew* I was on this earth.

I *knew* I was part of the human race, and I could fucking prove it!

All the doubts I had tried to sort out all my life and never could were immediately sorted out for me when I breast-fed that baby for the first time.

I *am* a human being.

I am not a figment of my imagination.

I am not an out-take.

I exist!

I really exist!

Christian Peppard gave me my existence, and that made it possible for me to give myself my life.

The debt I owe him I'm not sure he'll ever understand. I'm not sure I'll ever be able to explain it to him much less repay it. But I know I am indebted to him in a way most women are not indebted to their children.

From the moment he was born, I owed him for my existence. The fact of his birth gave me a strength I'd always lacked, that I'd never been able to find.

He legitimized my life.

He came with strong love.

When the nurse came back to take Christian, I didn't want to let him go. I couldn't get enough of him. George felt the same way. He loved that child with all the love that was in him. I never saw him so happy.

100

George knew a lot about babies because he'd had babies before. I knew nothing. And he was able to enjoy Christian in a way he never could his other children when they were infants. When Brad and Julie were born, George was young and out of work and tormented with worry about how he was going to support them.

Through an accident of nature Christian gave us almost all the up side of a baby and none of the down. He ate when he was supposed to eat. He slept when he was supposed to sleep. He rarely ever got sick. The few times he ran a fever, we bathed him in alcohol and he immediately responded the way he was supposed to. He was easy and cheerful and funny, and neither of us could keep our hands off him.

Christian was five months old when George decided it was time for him to be weaned, which meant he also thought it was time for me to be weaned.

Little by little I substituted the bottle for my breast. Christian didn't have a bit of trouble with the change. He would eat anything that was stuck in his mouth, wherever it came from.

I didn't find it quite that easy. I did what George told me, but I wasn't really ready to stop nursing my baby. It seemed so strange to remove the milk from my body with the rubber suction cup. For the first time in over a year I began to get depressed. My anxiety demon returned from vacation, and I blamed George for it. Looking back, I realize he was right. I might easily have become one of those women who depend upon their children for their entire existence. George was very aware that we were both neurotic, unstable people and didn't want to lay that on our kid. He knew Christian was bound to get enough of that for free.

He explained that I couldn't keep running to the crib and picking Christian up every time he cried. There were times I'd have to let him holler unless I wanted a child who would demand instant gratification for the rest of his life.

That was hard, but I did it.

I'd go down the list whenever he started bitching. Was he wet? Was he hungry? Was there a pin sticking through his diaper? Did he need to be burped or turned over? If none of the above, then he just wanted more attention and I had to let him be.

I would stand out in the hallway, peeking in from the crack in the door, fighting every impulse in me to run to him, repeating over and over again to myself, "You can't go in there. You can't go in there."

George announced he was taking me off to Palm Springs. Just the two of us. Christian had to stay home.

It was time to be a wife again.

London, 1969

6

The rules of the game are not structured to produce an artist. They are structured to produce a star for profit. They are not structured for achievement. They are structured for success. And if you have it in you to become an artist, if you have it in you to achieve, there comes a time when being a star and a success are revealed as empty and meaningless by themselves. They cannot make you happy in your work. And if a performer is not happy in his work, he can never be happy in his life.

The birth of our baby didn't dispel George's torment. It only diverted him from it for a while. Even when I was pregnant in Rome and everything seemed so wonderful, he still had to report to work every day and fight the fights that can never be won.

When I joined George in Rome he had already been over there a month. It was now the middle of winter, but the production called for two weeks of night shooting outdoors. They tell you you're supposed to sleep during the day, but you never can. George was too busy working on the rewrites to try to make the script a little bit better. He was exhausted, then he became sick and feverish with the flu.

One night during the break he happened to see what the crew was being given to eat for dinner. The men were doing hard physical labor in the middle of the night and it was freezing cold, but all the company had provided was cold box lunches—a piece of fruit, a slice of day-old bread, and a hunk of salami. Unlike many above-the-title people, George just couldn't ignore it or pretend he didn't notice as he headed past to the warmth of his trailer and the nice hot meal that was waiting for him.

He hunted down the unit manager, some Yugoslavian who wound up owning a block of the Via Veneto after working on *Cleopatra*. George said, "Uh-uh, those men get hot food. You can't do the kind of work they have to do without hot food."

The unit manager was put off by the intrusion on his turf, but since George was the star he masked his irritation with a cynical shrug.

"Well, I don't see how that's going to be possible. The company won't pay for it. It's not in the budget." Then with a worldly smile, "Besides, that's what they're used to."

George was furious.

"Fuck that! I'll pay for it!"

The next night the hot food was there. The crew wouldn't touch it. George couldn't understand why, and no one would tell him. Finally, when he was standing by himself, one of the men took him aside and explained what was going on.

"We eat any of that food and we don't work any more. That's what the boss told us."

George was unable to accept that.

"Oh, really? Well, we'll just see about that."

The man begged him to let it be.

"Please, Mr. Peppard, don't say anything. The boss is very hard. He'll fire us, and he'll hurt you too. I'm serious. He can do it. He'll have you shot in the street."

George isn't the kind of person who can back off from something like that, and he began to obsess on it. It exhausted and drained him even beyond the point where he was already exhausted and drained. It sickened him in every sense of the word, to the point where he

105

had a fever of 103 and was pissing blood. I watched the doctor give him a shot that would knock out an elephant to keep him from going to the set, and then give him another one when that wasn't enough.

The next day I had to wake George up to take a transatlantic call from Universal back in Beverly Hills. They said they knew he wasn't on the set because he'd been drinking. The lawyers were drawing up an edict against him. If he didn't get back to work immediately, they would file charges.

That's the sort of thing that happens time and time again. It's so far past rational understanding, so past anything that makes sense, that the only thing you can do is become deranged.

As long as George still had the ranch he was able to feel it was all for something. But it became harder and harder to keep coming up with that $700,000 in cold cash every year that would make it finally viable. He wasn't Howard Hughes. He was an actor.

Over the next few years he became more and more exhausted from working his butt off doing junk movies in Europe so he could send the money back home to make the ranch go. And he became more and more frustrated and disillusioned from hating the kind of pictures he had to do. There were no good scripts, no good directors, and at some point it became icily clear that there weren't going to be any. The way the system works, you can't really fight the studios. The business managers and the lawyers and the studio honchos are always in bed together. The studios know what your debts are. You can't keep it a secret. So they have you. They had him.

It was an impossible situation at best. Then a run of bad luck made it even worse. There were two years of

106

drought, and George had to undertake the enormous additional expense of putting in an irrigation system. When he flew up to the ranch to see for himself how the work was progressing, he discovered the ranch manager was incompetent and had let the whole place slide down the tubes.

It got to be too much. One day he came home from a business meeting and told me he was putting the ranch up for sale. He couldn't hold on any longer.

George became a man possessed. He was trying so hard to fix his life, but everything he attempted seemed to come back on him in some terrible way. It was like getting whiplash from your dreams.

He kept looking to me for solace and support. I couldn't give them to him. I felt my only choices were either to lie to him and tell him what he needed to hear or tell him the truth and hurt him more. Neither alternative was tolerable. I saw him keep trying to make things work in his movies that there was no way to make work, and I wanted to say, "George, say the line and hit the mark, and leave it there." But I knew that to his credit and despair he could never do that, so I said nothing. I wanted to say, "Hell, man, I don't need to be rich. The fur coats, the Mercedes-Benz, the house in Beverly Hills—that's all bullshit." But I knew he couldn't deal with that either.

I felt helpless. There was nothing I could do, nothing I could say that would make it better for him.

By the last year of our marriage, I was past caring.

We were back in London for yet another picture, and George had reached the point where he was tormented and angry every minute of the day. When you are angry like that you are really shaking your fist at the gods, but

107

since the gods don't answer, you take it out on whoever is around. I was around.

I understood why he began to ridicule and humiliate me, why he would sit me in a chair for hours at a time and take me apart, telling me I wasn't a good mother, I wasn't a good wife, I wasn't a good anything.

I understood his remorse the next day when he would try to make me feel better by telling me it wasn't my fault I couldn't make him happy. And I understood why that only made me feel worse.

But you can only live with a man who is enraged and despairing and desperately unhappy for so long, and then it no longer matters why.

I started to hate him.

I felt demoralized, weak, helpless, and afraid. I was long past arguing or fighting or even talking. I closed down and became like a vegetable. All I wanted to do was stay out of his way. I had trouble thinking past one day to the next, but I knew I was trapped. I had a baby, and there was no way for me to get out. The only thing I could do was play with my child.

One afternoon I returned to the house from watching the changing of the guard at Buckingham Palace with my baby when George called me from the Dorchester Hotel. It was his day off and he'd had lunch with Joan Collins, who had gotten in that morning for the picture. Now he was up in her hotel suite with Samantha Eggar, Guy Mac-Ilwaine, and some other members of the Dorchester set. It was the very last place in the world for him to be. You only hang out with that hard, fast crowd if you are in control, very strong, and totally on top of it. If you're strung out, if you're drunk, if you're upset, they are on it in a second like dogs on a bone. And George was just all great raw soul.

I heard the manic euphoria in his voice as he ordered me to come over there. He'd been drinking.

I said, "George, please, I don't want to come to the Dorchester. I want to stay home by myself."

Sometimes there is nothing lower or more of a joke than a movie star's wife. I didn't need any further humiliation.

George was insistent. I could hear them giggling and laughing in the background as he pressured me.

"Don't be jealous. Come on over. I'm sending the car around."

Click. He hung up.

Now I was not only the movie star's wife but the jealous movie star's wife, a joke within a joke. "Jealous?" I'd have been grateful if he'd found somebody else. I prayed he would have an affair or get himself a trick.

Ten minutes later the driver was at the door. I got in the car. I was afraid not to. It would only postpone the inevitable scene and make it worse.

When I walked into the room, George jumped up and introduced me with an exaggerated flourish.

"Ladies and gentlemen, this is my wife. She doesn't like me much. But this is my wife."

As far as they were concerned, I wasn't even there.

I didn't bother to take off my coat. I knew he had to shoot the next day, and I could see how they were treating him, like some kind of boring, unwelcome drunk who had crashed their party.

I tried to hide my emotion when I spoke.

"George, I'm leaving. I think you should come with me."

He said, "You don't go *anywhere* without my say-so," and then he laughed.

For the first time in years, something in me said, "No, this kind of humiliation I will not take. I will not play the out-of-control movie star's wife, who everybody hopes can scrape him out of here and take him home."

George had brought me there to play just that part,

only his scenario was different. The way his read was: "You *can't* get me out of here!"

They had made him feel powerless and stupid and foolish, so he was going to demonstrate in front of them all that he had power over some living thing, and it was going to be me. He was going to make me come to heel. I had already been brought to heel quite a lot.

I said, "I'm going, George. You come with me or you stay. I don't really give a shit which you do!"

When I got downstairs, I told the driver to stick around and try to get him home, then I took a cab back to the house.

For the first time since I had been married, I knew I had to get it together by myself. Maybe I didn't matter, but my baby did. I sat down on the couch with a pad of paper and a pack of cigarettes and started trying to figure out the options for my life. What were my possibilities? What were my weaknesses? Where were my strengths? .

Hours later the driver brought George back and put him to bed. But I continued to sit there through the night, totaling it up to see where it all came out. The bottom line was bleak, but at least it was something.

I had to leave him. Trying to stick it out wasn't going to change anything or make it any better. I'd done enough sticking it out. I couldn't stand it any more.

Okay, where do you go?

There was nothing for me in London, not even any friends of my own. Everyone I knew had something to do with George, and they weren't even *his* friends, just people he worked with. The house in California was rented, so I couldn't go there. It had to be New York.

All right. Now, what are you going to do in New York?

I would have to go back to work. I would have to try to be an actress again.

110

The answer terrified me. I had no ambition. I had no confidence. I didn't even know if I could get a job. But no matter how I added it up, I kept returning to it. It was my only shot, the only way I could possibly get back up on my own two feet.

I was fighting for some last shred of dignity and knew I could never have it as long as George was supporting me. When we were still communicating enough to argue, he would say, "Sure, you'll leave me and take everything I've got, just like all the other Hollywood wives." I'd scream at him, "Goddammit, George, how can you say that to me? I was never in this for the money, and you know it!" He never believed me. At least he said he didn't. I had to show him I meant it. Otherwise, he could malign me, humiliate me, and ridicule me to the world and I would have no recourse. A woman never does as long as she's dependent on someone else to pay her way.

When he came out of the bedroom the next morning I was still afraid, but I was ready for him. I watched him drink his coffee, then I said, "I want to talk to you. There's something important you have to hear."

He said he didn't feel like it now. Maybe later.

It had been a long time since we had spoken civilly to each other.

I said, "You never have to talk to me again, but you have to talk to me now because I'm leaving you. I'm going to New York. I'm taking Christian. I'm not sure what I'll do, but I can't make this any more."

He railed at me. Then he cried. Then he made promises. But I had been through all that before. I was starting to get tough.

"That's it, George. I mean it. I'm going."

As soon as he left the house I picked up the phone and made the plane reservations. That afternoon Christian and I took a cab to the airport and flew to New York.

The next week I was sitting in David Susskind's office talking about a part in a television special he was producing. The day I hit town I had called my old theater agent and said, "Hi, Stark, it's me. I'm back. Think you can get me some kind of work?" He sent me over the script for the Susskind show, and I read it just as fast as I could tear it out of the envelope. It was terrible, a comedy about welfare. I hadn't seen Susskind since I was a kid, and as I sat there holding forth about how, well, yes, I'd read the script and hadn't liked it much, he broke into a big smile, then said exactly the right thing.

"You chickenshit. You haven't worked in six years. You don't know if you can cut it again. Don't tell me about the script isn't good. Any job you can get is the job you should take. You're just scared."

I thanked him for keeping me honest. He was absolutely right. I *was* scared, scared to death.

He offered me the part, and I took it. And I didn't do too badly with it, either, which gave me the beginning of some kind of confidence.

Three months later I scored a second job in a television movie called *Harpy*. While I was on location outside of Fresno, California, I had my first affair since I'd gotten married.

It had never occurred to me to run around on George while we were still together. If it had, I would have been too afraid to do anything about it. George was so full of anger that he was just looking for an excuse to take a gun to somebody.

But after I left him, he started sleeping with a young English actress in his picture, and he made sure I knew all about it. The gossip columns were full of it the way they are only when somebody is telling. You get to know how to read between the lines. I assumed George was feeding them all the juicy tidbits for my benefit. They had the desired effect. He always wanted me to be jealous, and I never was. Now after all those years he finally got to me. The girl was blonde and pretty and a lot younger than me.

What blew me out was that at the same time he was shacked up with her he was writing me long, soul-searching love letters about how he was sure we could make it if we both tried. I was just starting to go for it when the gossip began to hit the papers. Perhaps unreasonably, I felt horriby betrayed. Once again he had put me in a place of public embarrassment and humiliation.

I thought, "Oh, please, just leave me alone. The hell with you. I'll have an affair of my own if there's some man somewhere who still finds me attractive."

There was—a young actor on *Harpy* named Tom Nardini. We spent all the hours we weren't shooting having a wonderful time getting stoned, riding horses, and running around in the fields barefoot in our jeans. It couldn't have been better.

I was still on location when I received a telegram from George. He was on his way back from London and would be coming to see me in a couple of days. I figured he'd call after he got home, but as soon as he landed in Los Angeles he hired a private plane and flew up to Fresno in the middle of the night. I suppose he was trying to catch me fooling around. He almost succeeded. I was shacked up wih Nardini when he walked into the motel.

Thank God, the hairdresser on the picture spotted him as he strode through the lobby and asked the desk clerk for Mrs. Peppard's room. They didn't have a Mrs. Peppard listed and he refused to ask for Miss Ashley, so while he was hassling that out with the clerk she got on the house phone and called me at Nardini's place. "Peppard is in the lobby!"

I beat it back to my room just seconds before George knocked on the door. He walked in, put down his briefcase, looked at the unused bed and said, "All right, who have you been fucking?"

I wanted to kill him. Literally. I had gotten one leg back up as a human being, and in that flash of an instant he somehow came to represent everything that had ever stopped me, everything that had ever made me afraid.

I lunged for his briefcase to get at the loaded gun I knew would be there. He came straight at me, and I picked up the case and struck him with it hard enough to stun him, then snapped it open and grabbed at the gun, a huge .357 Magnum. I was crazed and I was going to blow him away. He smacked me on the arm, and when the gun went flying out of my hand he made a dive for it and got it back.

That's how we said hello.

An hour later we were reconciled. I'm still not sure why. I suppose it was the last bit of self-destructiveness left in me. But I said, "I have got to work. I mean, no shit about it. Up front, I have *got* to work." He said, "Okay," and I went back with him.

The part about working was the first to go.

Two months later I was on location in Laguna for *Marriage to a Young Stockbroker* when George called late in the afternoon.

"Can you talk?"

His voice sounded cold and distant.

"Sure, I'm finished shooting for the day. What's up? Anything wrong?"

He let me have it with both barrels.

"Your son almost died today while his mother was on location."

George's Aunt Mary had been taking care of Christian while he played around the swimming pool. She went inside the house for a moment, and when she came back out he was floating unconscious in the pool with a large gash on his brow. He must have slipped and hit his head on the edge, then fallen in. Thank God George was home because Mary couldn't swim. He ran from the house when he heard her scream, then pulled Christian out and brought him around with mouth-to-mouth resuscitation.

I drove back from Laguna faster than the speed of sound. What greeted me was that my kid had all but died because I wasn't there and that's what being an actress will do for you. No matter how rational you are, that one has to get you.

I said, "Okay, it's obviously a mistake for me to work. You cannot work and have a child at the same time. That's been made patently clear."

I finished up the picture and stopped working again, and from then on out it was like an armed camp. I lived under the same roof with him and kept up appearances in public, but that was it. Forget trying to get along. I slept by myself in the room next to Christian and lived for the days his father would be out of town. And my terrific laughing child wasn't laughing quite so much any more.

George and I had somehow invested all our salvation in each other and neither of us was saved, so we hated each other for it, which is the way it goes. But for whatever reason, we both felt compelled to play the movie out to the final scene. It wasn't long in coming.

I had a gay friend move in as a house guest to take some of the pressure off. George was drinking a lot now, and I was afraid to be alone with him. He took to waking me up in the middle of the night, saying, "I want to eat. Get up and cook something." It was like training a dog. I was enough of an automaton to do it. Anything, just so I didn't have to talk to him.

One night we came back from a charity party close

to four in the morning. George had been drinking all evening. He told me he was hungry, so I went to the kitchen to make him an omelette. I turned on the light, put the iron frying pan on the burner, and was breaking the eggs in the bowl when he lurched into the kitchen and came straight at me. I tried to get out of his way, but he picked up the hot frying pan and swung it at me as hard as he could. It caught me right on the side of the face. He was totally out of control. I was sure he was going to kill me.

I ran screaming to the guest room, but the door was locked and my friend wouldn't let me in. Somehow I managed to get outside and into my car. I jammed it into gear and tore out of the driveway without looking back.

I drove around Beverly Hills until I found an outside phone booth. I needed some help and a place to go. My face hurt terribly. It was cold and the top was off the car. I only had on pants and a thin bare midriff blouse.

A hotel was out of the question. Someone might see me, and it would get out in the business. One of my eyes was closed and the whole side of my face was bruised and swollen. But if you are a movie star's wife, no matter what he does to you, you keep it in the family.

I woke up George's lawyer and told him what happened. I could hear his brain suddenly start to turn over through the sleepiness.

"Well, gee . . . Uh, sure, I guess you could come over, except we're leaving for Palm Springs in the morning and . . . Oh, you'll be okay. Don't worry about it."

"What am I supposed to do? Drive around Beverly Hills at four in the morning?"

"Oh, go on home."

"I can't go home by myself. I'm afraid of him."

His closing line was, "Remember one thing, Elizabeth. If you don't go home, he's got you on desertion."

116

I dialed George's agent. His answering service refused to put me through.

"He'll have to call you in the morning."

"He can't call me in the morning. I don't even know where I'll be in the morning. I've got to talk to him now."

"I'm sorry, Mrs. Peppard. He's sleeping and can't be disturbed."

None of George's people wanted to get involved.

Finally I called my friend Beverly Coburn.

She said, "Right! Come over immediately. You'll stay here."

"I can't, Beverly. My baby's there. I'm afraid to go back, but my baby's there."

"Okay, we'll get your baby. Tell me where you are. I'll be right there."

Five minutes later the headlights of her car turned the corner. She took one look at my face, and I didn't have to say another word.

When we got back to the house, I waited in the car until Beverly went inside and checked out the scene. She found George sitting in his office in the guest house by the pool, staring down at his desk. She gave him two Valiums, then made up the bed in the office, and told him to stay there for the night. I wouldn't go to sleep without Christian, so she brought him to my bedroom and placed him down next to me. He was still sleeping. I closed the door and locked it from the inside. Beverly slept on the living-room couch.

George woke up early the next morning full of apologies. I was hard and mean. The only thing I had to say was, "Get out. Just get out."

I threw my house guest out too. "A friend like you I don't need!" He seemed surprised I was angry. "Well,

I thought it was just a family row and I ought to mind my own business."

George went to stay at a friend's place. Two days later he called and said he had taken the veil. He was never going to touch another drink and wanted to come home.

Once more I said, "Okay."

That lasted about a week.

A few friends were over for dinner the night before George was to leave on a publicity tour for his new movie. We were sitting around the dining-room table when he poured himself just one drink and then just one more. Then he started in on me again.

"Why the hell isn't Christian toilet trained? Don't tell me he's only three years old. The kid still shits in his pants! If you were any good as a mother, you'd have that together!"

Nobody said a word. My dinner guests stared down at their plates. They had a lot to tell me when George wasn't around, but that didn't do me any good now.

George suddenly got up from the table and left the room. He stumbled back in with Christian in his arms. Christian was sleepy and crying. I automatically rose up from my chair to keep George from dropping him.

He snapped at me, "Sit down!"

I said, "I'm going to the bathroom."

I went into the bedroom and got out George's gun. I walked back to the dining room, came up behind him, and stuck the barrel hard up against the base of his skull.

"Give me that baby or I'll blow your head off! I'll kill you!"

I meant it, and he knew I meant it. I would have killed him gladly. I wanted the excuse. That's how much I hated him that moment. Not him, but the possessed, drained, raw, sick, disillusioned man he had become.

Holding the gun in one hand, I reached over with

the other and took Christian from him. Two of the men at the table grabbed hold of George and got him out to his office. I dressed my baby and packed up his clothes, then went off to Beverly Coburn's.

The next morning I left Christian with Beverly and drove back to the house by myself. I didn't need anyone to come with me this time. I was past being frightened.

I found George sitting on his bed packing his suitcase for the publicity tour.

"That's it," I told him. "It's all over."

He looked up at me and said, "You'll calm down by the time I get back. There's nothing you can do. Think about it."

I did think about it during the two weeks he was gone. I thought about it a lot. Then I found myself a lawyer.

George was wiped out when he came home and went straight off to bed. The next morning I waited for him to get up with a kind of calm clarity. When he came out of the bedroom I felt almost serene.

I said, "Here's some coffee. I'm getting a divorce. I don't want to talk about it. I don't want any scenes about it. I would like you to pack your things and get out of here until I can move into my own place."

I knew what he was going to say.

"Oh, no. I'm not leaving. If anybody's leaving it's going to be you. And you're not taking Christian with you either."

I was ready for it. I'd gotten mean. Real mean.

"George, there are witnesses who will give depositions. People have seen my eye, my cheek, my jaw. Either you find some place else to sleep or I will tell the papers that I am divorcing you because of assault and battery with a deadly weapon."

The next day he was gone.

It was finally over.

I spoke with George on the telephone last night. We talk all the time now, mostly about Christian but also about our work. Last night he told me about his new movie. He sounded so clear and happy. Maybe because for the first time it really is his movie. He's not just acting in it. He's also directing and producing, putting up every dollar himself.

As pictures go it's low budget, but he had to mortgage the house and everything else he owns to get the money together. He's going for it. He's really going for it. Maybe it will work and maybe it won't. It's always a crap shoot. But even if it doesn't and he loses the house and the cars and all the rest of it, he'll still come out ahead because he'll have done something of his own.

I understand so much more about the pressure he was under than when I was married to him, because now I have been under the same pressure myself. Maybe one of the reasons I've been able to make my life work moderately well is because of living with George. He taught me a lot about professionalism. I also had great training about what not to do, about what not to depend on, and what not to look to for solace and reward. I'm talking about the Business, the Wise Men, the Way Things Are Done, the Rules of the Game. Because if you live your life trying to abide by those things you only become "cooperative."

After I left George I never had any more questions about the right course of action to take in one's work.

I had seen what the Wise Men and the people in power can do to a performer.

I had seen how they use talent like toilet paper.

I had seen what happens to an actor who tries to change the system from within.

I had seen a good man and a strong man and a talented man driven to a state of demented hysteria.

And nobody could sell me the system after that. I didn't want to be on their turf.

All the fights and wars and male-female battles George and I fought are truly immaterial now. They involved things both of us had to work out for ourselves, and each of us found in the other the perfect partner to work them out on. We were both so full of rage and anger and pain. Both of us—not just me—were frightened people who didn't believe in ourselves very much, who were afraid we were nothing, counterfeit, no good.

And we didn't really end up too badly. The proof of that is in our child and the fact we are now finally able to like each other in a way that fits.

That was the problem. We loved each other, but it didn't fit.

I suppose that's what all the leavings and comings back, all the let's-try-one-more-times and my-God-I-can't-stand-it-anymores were about. We had to keep trying to find a way to make it fit. We wanted so desperately to love each other in some way that made us happy. And we did love each other, but there was no Yin and Yang. It didn't fit.

Now it does.

George and I were meant to know each other, be married, and have a child. We were never meant to be mated.

We come from different cultures and have different tastes.

We are both actors.

George wants a woman to cook and sew and stay home and have that be enough, to have his life be large enough for two. And that's legitimate. I want exactly the same thing in my life. I want to go out, do the work, and have the food waiting on the table when I get home.

Both people can't have that. I could never be married

121

to an achiever because I'm *the achiever. And I'm selfish about it. When I achieve I need somebody first of all to tell me I really did achieve and then tell me what was good about it. I don't have energy left over to become involved in someone else's achievement. I'm that selfish.*

I think most actors are.

Santa Monica, 1970

7

When I left George the only things I took with me were Christian and the furniture. The only money I wanted was what I came into the marriage with. I wanted to leave clean. Few movie-star wives do. Before the California divorce laws changed, a lot of them went into the marriage for the divorce.

It could be an ugly game. People in the business would look at the wives like pieces of raw meat hanging in the sun to be taken apart inch by inch with a cleaver. One of the favorite pastimes was betting on how long they could hang there before starting to turn putrid. And the women would go for it. They would put up with a lot of shit because they knew if they could hold out and get the old man to get it up enough to where they had the kid, fifty percent of everything he made for the rest of his life would be theirs, and maybe more.

I'd seen that happen a lot. My sympathy was always much more with the man. I didn't want any part of it.

I had no choice but to go back to work as a full-time professional. It was no longer a matter of ego or self-fulfillment or the odd job here or there. I needed the work to support myself so I could pay my own way.

I knew I had nothing going for me and the odds were all against me. I was thirty years old, an age when God knows women, particularly actor-ettes, are considered over the hill, and I'd already blown it once before.

Most of the heavyweights in the business didn't like me much, and they had their reasons. The first time around six years before I had been a loud-mouthed, smart ass, temperamental crazy lady, and I hadn't even been much good. I'd gotten real hot for a while, but when you're hot you're hot, when you're not you're not. The only difference really is that when you're hot everyone tells you how good you are, and when you're not hot any more they let you know you never were worth a shit.

I called my old movie agent.

"Well, Herman, George and I are getting divorced. I need to go back to work."

There was silence on the other end.

"Look, I'm not dumb enough to think I'm going to be a movie star. I'm old laundry and I know it. But I'm going to earn my living and I'm going to earn it by doing what I know how to do, and that's perform. Not with the high rollers maybe, maybe not even in the movies. I'll go be somebody's wife in a television series or something."

He said, "Sweetheart, I think you better reconsider that divorce. I don't think I can even get you a guest shot on *Bonanza*. I doubt if I ever will. You're smelly fish in this town."

It flashed through my mind that maybe George still didn't want me to work, and if he didn't I wouldn't, at least not in California. Yet I had to stay there. According to the custody agreement, I'd lose Christian if I established residence out of state, and I had already used most of my money as down payment on a small house in Santa Monica.

I thought about all those actresses who married stars and stopped working, then weren't able to come back again after the divorce. It's easy to say, well, they're too old now; they've been off the screen for too long; they never were that good to begin with. But you wonder about them. Why can't they get any jobs? Who is it that's mad at them?

125

The first thing I figured out was I'd better get myself another agent. I may have been full-tilt-boogie washed up, old, wasted, and over with, but performing was still the only thing I could do. I remembered a young agent at IFA who for some reason had said he wanted to represent me. I called him that afternoon and told him about my earlier conversation. He said he'd be happy to take me on.

The next thing I had to do was begin to get my chops up so I could handle the work if and when it came. Forget about walking. I was having trouble with the crawling part. I drove over to the Actors Studio and signed up for my friend Lou Antonio's acting exercise class.

For the first time in my life I started consciously trying to learn my craft and explore the art of acting. I didn't care if I was successful. I didn't care if I was recognized. I didn't care about the politics or the career. I needed to work, and I knew that the only real strength an actor has is his skill as a performer.

When I got up in the morning I'd have breakfast with Christian on the back-door steps of my house. There was an old peach tree in the yard, and Christian would pull down the ripe peaches he could reach, then I'd cut them up and put them in a bowl with heavy cream and we'd sit there in the sunshine eating. Then I'd leave Christian with Christine, a wonderful woman I firmly believe was Heaven-sent to be my guardian angel. To keep things straight between me and the Lord. Then I'd drive over to the Actors Studio for an afternoon of classes.

All the while I kept waiting for the phone to ring, hoping it would be my agent saying he had something for me.

Slowly the jobs started coming in. I did guest shots on *Ironside* and *The Six Million Dollar Man* and *Love American Style* and *Marcus Welby*. For an actor, those

126

are some of the lowest gigs there are, but I did them all and did them as well as I could. I had to come face to face with a difficult truth. "Look," I told myself, "I don't know if I'm any better than this material. But hell, man, it's an honest job, and I'll go and do an honest day's work." I treated each job with respect, which wasn't hard because I did have respect for it. I was grateful every time I got a part because it meant I could make my house payment and that my kid and Christine and I were okay.

There were also times I had to go up and read before ex-used-car salesmen from Van Nuys who didn't know who I was, and that was hard. There was still a part of me that never forgot that I had starred on Broadway and had won a Tony Award and a Drama Critics Award and a Laurel Award. Not that those things mean very much, but it wasn't as if I was some model who had never stood on a stage before.

One day I went to read for a small part in a movie, and when I walked into the producer's office there must have been a dozen other actresses sitting in the reception room waiting to audition.

The secretary looked up from her *Cosmopolitan* and handed me a script.

"Here, read this. They'll call you when they're ready."

That had never happened to me before, even when I was a kid just starting out. But I wanted the job, so I sat down and waited.

Finally, my turn came and I went in for the interview.

The producer checked me up and down, then said, "Oh, yeah, didn't you used to do stuff a long time ago? Weren't you in some series or something?"

That really got to me. I couldn't help myself. I rolled the script up and shoved it back at him.

127

"Do I have to tell you what to do with it? If you want my credits, look in *Who's Who in the American Theatre!*"

That's the sort of thing that makes you humble. If you've never learned humility before, you learn it then. Because in the carnival there is very little grace when you're low. A bareback rider has grace when she's on the horse, but not when she's trying to get up on it. And there's no forgiveness. And there's no compassion. And there's no understanding. Because failures stink. Nobody wants to be around you. Nobody wants to know you. And nobody will tell you the truth. Because if they did tell you the truth, they would have to tell you something about themselves that they don't want to know. We're all really in it together; that's the part that sticks up everyone's ass.

I didn't want their success. I'd been there. Maybe a part of me did want it, but it was a desire I knew was the devil. I didn't respect it. I knew what it was. I'd seen the face of the devil. I'd been fucked by the devil. I'd fucked the devil. We'd given each other head. That's when you know the devil. It's not something you have to remind yourself about. It's with you every day of your life.

All I wanted was survive on the outside. At the age of thirty I finally began to figure out that that was my natural turf, the place where I'm supposed to be. God keeps telling you things and finally you listen. I was obviously a slow learner, but at last I began to catch on.

I took each job as it came, and I suppose whatever sense of dignity I'll ever have was born then.

It may only have been schlock television. There was no pressure on me to do anything more than show up, hit the mark, and say the lines. But I brought everything I had in me to each job and tried to use it as an acting exercise so I could get the most I could out of it.

It was like being a keyboard player in a bus-and-truck Lawrence Welk band working the lounge at the

Holiday Inn in Pacoyma. The music is only what it is, but maybe once a night a particular tune comes up where it wouldn't hurt anything to try out some chord changes or licks you've always wanted to play. In the same way, I would try to do a certain kind of sense memory in a particular scene or build a character to give it a little extra dimension.

Sometimes the director would go along with me, sometimes he wouldn't. When I played a hooker on an episode of *Police Story,* I wanted to show her really wasted, the way those ladies get to be after snorting coke and working with their backs to the open door for fifteen years. Los Angeles is full of them. The director only let me go ten percent of the way, but still that was ten percent more than what was called for.

The jobs started to come a little faster and got a little bit better and a little bit better. I began to get leads in movies for television as well as guest shots on other people's series. The movies were mostly dogs, but my own work was improving.

I was starting to get pretty good, mainly because I finally understood that all I wanted in my own work was to be able to perform and play myself the way Jimi Hendrix played the guitar, the way B. B. King sings the blues. That's art. Art isn't something you do or are. It's where you aim, the target you shoot at. And I knew that in a world where there was very little I could respect or even accept, it was the highest, most noble thing I could recognize. I guess that's what the Pope is supposed to feel about God. And if that is an illusion, it's an acceptable one for me.

And I began to discover that there were just as many people in the business who were kind and generous and giving as there were those who were the opposite. It was a shock to realize not all producers and businessmen were bad guys, but like everyone else in the world had to be dealt with as individuals rather than as companies, categories, slots, and titles.

I still had a lot of the old anger in me when I came back to work, and for years I was a biased, prejudiced producer hater. They were a poisoned breed for me, and I treated them like shit. I wouldn't even shake their hands when I went on the job. I wasn't difficult or temperamental, but I wasn't very pleasant either.

"Oh, you're the producer, the man who is paying me the money to do the job? Okay, I'm going to do the job better than you deserve. Now please get out of my way. I don't want to discuss how I'm going to play it or even what I'm going to wear. I don't want to talk to you. I don't even want to know you."

I treated a lot of them like that, and they didn't deserve it. They were getting somebody else's rage. I'm sure they didn't begin to understand what was bugging me, nor did I want them to understand it. They thought I was hostile and cold, and they were right. It wasn't fair. I was unjustifiably mean and nasty to a lot of men who didn't do anything but give me a job.

I'm still not completely over that one, but at some point I began to try to rid myself of my built-in prejudices. I'd say out front, hopefully with some degree of ironic humor so they would laugh along with me and maybe understand me a little better, "Well, you know, to an actor you guys are guilty until proven innocent. That is, after all, your job."

What turned it around for me was a *Mission Impossible* I did with a producer named Barry Crane. Crane directed the episode himself because the script was extremely complicated and he was worried about bringing the show in on schedule. He had set aside eight days for shooting instead of the usual six, but it was still a problem because this particular episode had to be carried by the guest people rather than the regulars and there was a lot of heavy emotional stuff in the script, which is never easy to play.

It was a huge acting assignment for me, the toughest part I'd gotten since I came back to work. I had to play both the leading character and someone else impersonating her. And I had to do a couple of scenes as a wasted drunk and a long monologue in which I broke down while going through a Gestalt therapy session. I got the part only because they had to have somebody who could cut it and of the actresses who could cut it there was no one else around still working that kind of gig. They couldn't get Jane Fonda or Faye Dunaway to do a *Mission Impossible*. They couldn't even get Tuesday Weld. So they got me.

It was the first time I had something I could really sink my teeth into, and I had to go for it. I didn't care if anyone noticed or not. I made up my mind I was going to be good.

I had never met Barry Crane before and he didn't know anything about me, but as soon as we started rehearsing he instinctively understood that it was important to me way beyond what it was to anyone else. It was a hit show, so it didn't really matter. Normally, when you do a series like that, you come in, have a few laughs, play your part, then go home and wait for the check. But Crane saw I was on about something, and he knew I wasn't putting up a front so he would think I was some kind of arty actress. He also knew that to turn in the sort of performance I was trying to give in only eight days is pretty impossible.

The tight shooting schedule was putting all kinds of time and money pressures on him, but right from the beginning he supported and encouraged me every way he could. So did everyone else on the show. Without my even realizing what was happening, they all began to rally around me.

When we came to my first drunk scene, Barry Crane said to me, "Miss Ashley, I would like to get this in one day, but I don't want you to get wrung out. You go sit in your dressing room and think about whatever you have to think about while I rehearse the other actors. I'll call you when we're ready."

We didn't have to talk about it, but he understood that my chops weren't up all that much yet; my juices weren't really flowing. I knew what to go for, but I was still rusty inside. I was having to bang at myself to get to those parts of me I needed to keep it true. I could have protected myself by being facile and doing what I knew would work, but I wanted to take the chance and go for the real stuff, and he was making it possible for me to do that.

I was struck by the quality of quiet on the set when they called me back out. It wasn't the usual, "Quiet on the set, please! Jesus Christ, can't we keep those hammers down!" It was just something in the air that came from the other actors. I needed them, and they were all right up for it.

We began shooting, and I could tell right away it was going to be a good take. We were almost at the end when we reached the part where I had to go into a drunken rage and start breaking everything in sight. I picked up a vase and threw it at Bill Smith, that fine actor who played Falcon Eddie on *Rich Man, Poor Man*. You have to be very careful about that sort of thing so nobody gets hurt, but I made a bad throw and the vase hit him hard in the eye and shattered all over his face. He was bleeding badly but kept on going without even missing a beat. He wasn't going to break that take for anything!

The next day I had to do my toughest scene, a long monologue in which I slowly fall apart as I talk about my life to a therapy group. It was written to be done in a single shot with the camera moving in closer and closer as I begin to dissolve, so I had to be totally up for it. As soon as we started I knew it wasn't going right. I didn't cut the take, but I could tell it wasn't happening. I could feel myself getting dry. I started to tighten up, which only made it worse.

Then very quietly, in a tone of voice that doesn't break your concentration or disturb anything, Barry Crane began to speak.

"Continue right on. Continue right on. Don't anybody move or I'll kill ya. Miss Ashley is going to take it from the top again."

He turned to the camera operator.

"How are we for reels? Are we going to have to reload?"

The cameraman said, "No, we just put in a full one."

"All right then, keep the camera on Miss Ashley and hold her in focus. She will perhaps take the entire reel. Miss Ashley, you go back and forth on this any way you please."

You never get that on series television. They don't have time for it, and it doesn't really matter. But Barry Crane was so into what I was trying to do that he was prepared to shoot the whole reel if he had to. He didn't care that I was a washed-up actress who had blown her career. He didn't care that I had been married to George Peppard and the papers were full of gossip about the divorce. I didn't have to explain anything to him. He saw a human being giving everything she had to the work and he was going to give that back any way he could. He was a producer, one of the people who took shit from me, but he was saying, "Yeah, do it! Do it! What do you need to do it?"

And I did it. I got it.

I was able to do what I had never done before and thought I never would, which was to be real and use myself so the truth could come out of me without a plan. I wasn't faking anything. There was no makeup on my face. I wasn't being cute or glib or technical. It was real. And it wasn't just vomiting either. Anyone can go out and vomit in front of people. I used the emotion artfully without wallowing in it, controlling the flow the way a painter controls the oils on his canvas.

When the scene ended everyone on the set—Barry Crane, the crew, the actors, the extras—broke into applause. The camera operator had tears in his eyes, and so did I. I had gotten to their feelings and moved them all.

Up to then, I had never been sure I actually had any real feelings. Now I knew that I did and that I was able to express them in my work. I did it! Me! That kind of emotional truth had never come out of me before. I was extraordinarily elated. I felt like Muhammad Ali.

It was only a *Mission Impossible,* but it allowed me to start believing in myself as an actress. I could believe in myself because I had actually done it. Not in a classroom exercise but on the line. In front of a camera. In a real work situation where they were paying me money.

I had delivered and delivered good, not just good enough for them to say, "Okay, take and print."

I went for the gusto and got it.

I did it all the way.

8

It was right after my thirty-fifth birthday when the call came in from my movie agent. The excitement in his voice told me immediately it wasn't just another television guest shot.

"Okay, Elizabeth, are you ready for this? How would you like your own series? I just got off the telephone with the people, and they're hot for you to do it."

I was more surprised than he was, but tried to hold it together long enough to ask some of the right questions.

"You mean they want me to do a pilot, don't you, John, and then see what happens?"

"No, not a pilot but twenty-three to air, firm!"

"Have you talked about the money?"

"Of course I've talked about the money. It's twenty thousand an episode."

"For a firm twenty-three episodes?"

"That's right. You get paid twenty thousand dollars times twenty-three even if it's a bomb."

I stretched for a piece of paper and tried to do the arithmetic as he told me the idea for the show. At the moment the exact figure was beyond me, but I could get close enough to see it was a hell of a lot, more than I had ever made even when I was hot. As for the series itself, it sounded like the same old stuff, neither better nor worse than the usual. But that's almost beside the point in that particular game.

I said, "John, you definitely have my interest. But I'm going to have to process it. I'll get back to you tomorrow."

What troubled me was I knew that when my kind of actress does a television series she pretty much throws in the towel forever. With all the scheduling pressures and energy demands coming down on you week after week after week, you may be able to do the job competently and maybe even a little better than that, but by the time you're done you won't have much left to give to something really good if and when you ever get a shot at it. It's like if Jimi Hendrix had played jingles for five years, he wouldn't have been able to go back to playing the way he used to in the sixth year. He also might not have died. On the other hand, he might have died sooner. Who really knows?

I played with the ambiguities all afternoon but kept coming back to the fact that I was thirty-five years old and had a child and wasn't getting any younger. I started thinking, "Oh, the hell with it. Make a smart move for once in your life. Get yourself straight. What is it that's so terrific that you're saving yourself for?"

I called John back the next morning and told him to start negotiating the contract.

The weeks went by as they hammered out one clause after another. It's all a game they play. I was beginning to get used to the prospect of the show if not exactly comfortable with it, when my friend Gary Lockwood came over to hang out for the evening. Lockwood is a man who has been around and is truly one of God's real good creatures. I wanted to hear what he'd have to say about the series, hoping of course he'd tell me I had done the only sensible, mature thing. When I finished the back story, he was silent for a moment then looked me straight in the eye and told me precisely what he thought about it.

"Well, Bessie, you'd make a lot of money, all right. But do you know what it's going to cost you?"

I nodded that I did.

"Okay, there's only one thing I want you to think about. You've paid hard dues, but maybe you ought to bet on yourself a couple more times around the track before you pack it in."

I did think about it after Lockwood left. I thought about it a lot. But I felt tired and wasn't sure I had that kind of courage. I'd gotten safe. And I wanted to come in from the cold. You get weary of tap-dancing after a while, even if you enjoy it. I had made my smart move and was going to stick with it.

The next day I received a call from Stark Hesseltine, my old theater agent who had found me back when I was a student at the Neighborhood Playhouse.

He said, "Elizabeth, I've just finished talking with Michael Kahn from the American Shakespeare Festival at Stratford, Connecticut. He wants to know if you'll come for the summer to do Maggie in *Cat on a Hot Tin Roof*. The money is about five hundred a week and all you can eat."

I was too confused to come up with a coherent answer. Tennessee Williams has always been like some kind of god to me. *Summer and Smoke* was the first play I ever saw and as much as anything was responsible for my becoming an actress. The only plays I ever read were Tennessee Williams plays. They were like reading about my own life. When *A Streetcar Named Desire* was revived in Los Angeles the year before, I wanted to be in it so badly I got crazy when the producer wouldn't even let me audition.

"Well, Stark, y'see, I'm going to do this television series and y'know . . ."

"Are you set?"

"No, but they're negotiating and, well, it's pretty much all worked out."

"Yes, I understand that."

I had to close it off. Another minute on the phone and I'd have gone for it.

"Look, Stark, just tell Michael Kahn no, okay? Just tell him thanks but I can't do it."

Two days later Stark called back.

"Michael Kahn says if you don't have it absolutely nailed down, he doesn't have to set the part for another three weeks and he'll wait. If there's any chance you might consider it, he'll wait."

I didn't want him to wait. I wanted it to go away. But it wouldn't go away. Call it ego or arrogance or vanity or anything you want, but I owed myself one, and the next time Stark called I said yes.

It was a great play by a great playwright, and I knew it was probably the last chance I would ever have to be an artist. If I didn't take it, I would be a third-rate television actress for the rest of my life, grateful if that made it possible to take care of my kid and own my own house and car without having to marry some guy to support me.

I bit the bullet and made the call to my movie agent.

"John, there's something I have to tell you."

"Oh, hi, Elizabeth. If it's about the clause on the residuals, don't worry. We're working it out, and I expect to hear from them later today. They're probably—"

"No, man, that's not it . . . Uh, look, I'm not going to do the series. I'm sorry, I really am, but that's what I have to tell you."

It was a hard phone call. John had gone on the line for me. He'd scraped me up when nobody else could sell a slice of my ass to a horny man.

He couldn't have been more beautiful.

"Okay, Elizabeth, don't worry. Do what you have to do. I love you. We'll pay the rent somehow."

I had only done two plays since I came back to work. One was something called *Ring Around the Bathtub* by Jane Trahey, the advertising lady. It opened and closed on Broadway in one night. (I told them to change the title. They wouldn't listen.) The other was Giradoux's *The Enchanted* at Kennedy Center in Washington. But I didn't have any apprehension about going into *Cat*.

I didn't know what the director or the production or the rest of the company would be like, but I did know that for one of the few times in my life I was cast absolutely right. The part was played well before. It will be played well again. But some things have your name on them. That one had my name on it.

If there was ever a role my whole life summed up into, it was Maggie. I knew her inside and out, down to the marrow of her bones and the stream of her consciousness. She was Southern just like me, and her values and attitudes were all the same ones I grew up with.

She was a delta queen in love with a jock, a woman who knows from her upbringing how to sit down and chit-chat with the old folks in the most high-country-club ladylike way, and then go out to a road house, drink beer and boogie. That was the style where I came from.

She was also someone whose family had good social lines but no money. Her speech in the first act about what it was like to grow up a poor relation and dress in hand-me-downs could have been lifted from my own life.

I also saw something I think a lot of people not from the South had missed, which is that Maggie is wildly funny and funny in a specifically Southern way. Her sense of the ludicrous begins with herself, then extends to everyone and everything else around her. The entire first act is practically a monologue in which she dishes up one funny story after another. I know how to talk that talk. I cut my teeth on it.

140

The one thing I thought might give me trouble was Maggie's sexuality.

Like a lot of Southern women, her whole identity is based on being beautiful, sexual, and desirable. She has a lot of vanity—which is no bad thing in that part of the country—and when her husband won't go to bed with her it drives her into a frenzy. She becomes like an animal in heat, full of raw hunger and lust. That's the key to her character and the thing that makes the play work. I realized that if I was going to do her justice I would have to get down to the wail and the cry of a lowdown dirty blues song. That's what Maggie is, a ballsout lowdown blues song. It moans.

There was only one way for me to do that. Anything else would be cheating. I had to bring my own private animal lust out of the closet and expose it on the stage.

I'd never done that before, not in a movie or play or anywhere else in public. I was too insecure, so I had always been very antisexual in my work, playing everything against the sex. But now it had to be exposed, and that's hard to do, especially if you have locked away that part of yourself almost totally.

To make the play go, I had to give every man in that audience a hard on. But I'd never been a sexual exhibitionist. I'm not a woman who knows how to walk into a room and turn on every male in the place. There's really only one way to accomplish that, and that's when you're doing sex all the time and you want it so badly and love it so much it hangs all over you, like a smell. You have to be so into it that when you don't get it, it makes you crazy.

Ten minutes into the first act Maggie is down on her knees in her underwear begging for it. That was something else I had never been able to do. I'd had lots of scenes with lots of men, but I had never been able to beg for it. Whenever I got to the place where I wanted it that badly,

141

I split. I learned that from the couple of times I didn't split fast enough.

The problem took care of itself when I met McGuane.

After I signed the contract for *Cat* there was a six-week wait before rehearsals started in Connecticut, so when I was offered a part in *Rancho Deluxe* I took it. The script for the movie had a funny, off-the-wall quality that appealed to me. It was written by one Thomas McGuane, the same man who had written *The Sporting Club,* a novel I had also liked a lot. But mainly I thought the gig would be fun. It was being shot on location in Livingston, Montana, an old frontier town, and it would give me a chance to catch up with some friends I hadn't seen for a while. The cinematographer was my old buddy Billy Fraker, and the director was Frank Perry, a lovely man who produced the first play I ever acted in professionally when I was twenty years old.

The movie had already been shooting for three weeks the night I arrived in Livingston to begin my part. I checked into the motel with Christian and Christine, then ambled over to the little empty store across the street where Perry was showing the dailies. You always feel a bit strange when you first get on a movie location, but I never like to push my presence. People are working too hard to put out a welcoming committee for you, and the dailies are a good place to meet everyone in a relaxed way and pick up on the vibes of the production.

The store was filled with all the people in the company and just about everyone from town, most of whom had been hired on as extras. There was a lot of beer and laughter, and it was all happy and loose, the way dailies ought to be but seldom are.

After we said our hellos and I began to settle in, I

looked around and spotted this wild man in cowboy boots and jeans talking intensely to a young girl over in the corner. He was well over six feet tall with thick black hair hanging all the way down to his waist. There was something hard and mean about his face, but he also had huge, round, hound-dog eyes and a lovely warm grin. He wasn't a pretty man, not a man everyone would look at twice, but he definitely got my visceral attention.

I sidled over to Fraker and asked, "Who's that?"

Fraker said, "Oh, that's Thomas McGuane, our writer."

I wasn't looking for a location romance, but I thought, well now, that is certainly interesting.

Later that evening I talked with him a couple of minutes and liked him immediately. I sidled back to Fraker and said, "What's his story?"

People in the movies are quick, and Fraker got right to the point.

"Married."

"Gotcha. Pass."

I had never in my life been involved with a married man. It's not the kind of drama that appeals to me. I don't like lying and sneaking around and all the intrigue you have to put up with when no one is telling anyone else the truth. I also know that when a man is screwing around on his wife, it usually has more to do with his wife than it does with you.

Fraker read my disappointment and threw back his head and laughed.

"You mean I'm finally going to get a clear shot at it?" he teased.

"Fraker, you old wetback dandy, you've always had a clear shot at it. There was never a day when you didn't have a clear shot at it. You're just too much of a gentleman to make your move." That's the way we've talked to each other for fifteen years.

The next day was a day off, and everyone in the company drove out to McGuane's place, the Raw Deal Ranch, to hang out and loosen up. *Rancho Deluxe* was the first movie script he had produced, and he'd somehow managed to get it shot in his own back yard. As soon as I walked through the door a blonde young woman came up to me and shook my hand.

"Elizabeth! I'm Becky McGuane. How are you?"

She was all high energy, bright blue eyes and smiles, about the prettiest and warmest lady I'd ever met. Right from that second I adored her. She introduced Christian to her son, Thomas, who was also six years old, and when the two of them began to play, she took me into the kitchen where I helped her with the big pots of food she had cooked up for the afternoon. By the time we got the food out into the living room, we had become friends.

Becky was funny and warm and bright, everything I like in a person. She was almost enough to make me forget about her husband. Still, every time McGuane got within five feet of me I broke out into a lather. I couldn't quite figure it out. That just doesn't happen unless the attraction is mutual, yet it was perfectly obvious that he and Becky adored each other. There was no question that they had a terrific relationship.

I watched McGuane run his action over the course of the afternoon and saw there was also no question that he was an outrageous womanizer, flirting openly with every woman in sight. There was nothing idle about any of it, yet it didn't seem to bother Becky in the least. That made the two of them all the more interesting to me. I had spent years of my life wrestling with territorialism, and these people seemed to know something I didn't. Not that I had any intention of getting involved with McGuane. That's not how I ran my act.

It got to be night, and about fifteen of us jammed into a camper and drove to the Old Saloon, a bar out on the highway. Whether by accident or design, I was stuffed in next to McGuane. As we bounced along thigh by thigh, I watched my sexual frenzy do battle with my resolve.

If in the privacy of my own room I could have written a description of everything I wanted in a man right then —not what I wanted to want but what really turned me on, what I really liked and thought was fun—it would have come out Tom McGuane.

He was smart and funny and fast. He could give you the back story on something in four words. He could tell you some of the best outlaw stories you ever heard, then in the next paragraph discuss Turgenev.

That's just my style.

He was a writer.

I have always had a weakness for writers.

He was a psychedelic cowboy.

That's right up my alley.

He was a gonzo raver.

I love them the best.

He was an aging juvenile delinquent.

So was I.

But he was also trouble, and I was trying to get my life into a place where I didn't get into trouble for fun any more.

I was playing pinball with Christian when McGuane grabbed me by the arm and pulled me aside.

"Let's talk."

"Okay."

"Outside."

"Right."

He steered me out to the parking lot and into the cab of somebody's pickup truck, then stubbed out his cigarette in the ashtray and turned to face me.

"Let's fuck."

"What?"

"I said let's fuck."

Quite an opening, I thought, for one of America's primo young artists of the written and spoken word.

"I understand your meaning. I don't fuck married men. I adore your wife."

"We don't have that kind of scene."

"It's uncool."

"Not with Becky. Not with me."

Very sure of himself he was.

"I've never screwed a married man in my life. And if I were going to start, it certainly wouldn't be in his home town with his wife and kid around."

"I screw everybody. All the time. Becky and I screw all the time. She's crazy about you. So am I. It's okay."

"No, I don't think so. It's not my scene. But I hope we can flirt a lot and hang out and get to be pals because I think you're terrific. If you weren't married to Becky, I'd be on my back this minute."

"We'll talk more. Let's dance."

We climbed out of the pickup and went back into the bar and boogied.

The next day after work I ate dinner with Christian and Christine, then drove back to the Old Saloon to hang out for an hour or two. I was sitting at the bar drinking beer and talking with the guys when I spotted McGuane stride through the door and head straight toward me. I was, of course, looking for him. That's why I was there. But at the same time I hoped he wouldn't show.

He sat down on the stool next to me. The only thing I could think to do was slide a quarter over to him.

"Here. Why don't you go on over to the jukebox and play a tune."

"I don't take requests."

He laughed out loud, then pulled me off into a corner and got right down to it the way only a poet can.

"I want to fuck you so bad I'm not going to take no for an answer."

I looked at him and said, "Why? Do you have money on it?"

That seemed to set him back for a moment.

"Why would you think I had money on it?"

"Because as soon as the new actress arrives on the location, everyone makes bets about who's going to screw her. And you seem to me to be a man who needs to win a bet."

He smiled that big grin, but there wasn't much mirth in it.

"Are you really that tough?"

Tough? God, I was melting into the floor.

"No. I'm scared to death."

"Me too."

We spent the night in his camper in the parking lot behind the motel. Just before dawn he got up and went home.

I was up on a horse the next morning, rehearsing for a scene we'd be shooting that afternoon, when I saw Becky wave and head toward me.

"Elizabeth! Hi, Elizabeth!"

I considered galloping off to Los Angeles. Instead, I waved back and rode over to meet her.

147

"Hey, Elizabeth, how you doin'? Can you break for a couple minutes and take a walk with me. I want to talk to you."

"Uh, sure."

Oh, Christ, I thought as I climbed down. Here we go.

Becky looked positively radiant.

"Elizabeth, Thomas told me all about last night, and I think it's wonderful. Usually he just screws those dumb cowgirl teenyboppers."

For one of the few times in my life I was speechless.

"He has the biggest crush on you, but he told me at breakfast he's afraid you won't have anything more to do with him because of me. It may sound real strange, but I want you to know it's absolutely no infringement on where I live. We've been married a long time and don't have those kinds of jealousies. I really do approve."

I stopped walking and looked her hard in the face to make sure I had heard her right.

She laughed and said, "No, it's really fine."

I said, "Becky, I'm going to have to run that one by. You've got to understand, I'm not looking for a man. I'm not even looking for a love affair. But I do have this lather of lust for him."

"And he has it for you. If I ever saw two people who are supposed to know each other, it's you and Thomas. So whether you do it or don't do it, don't *not* do it because of me. Okay?"

She gave me a big reassuring hug, and I hugged her back.

"Becky, you're a far-out lady."

At the age of thirty-five I began the love affair I had wanted to have even before I knew what a love affair was. I didn't think it was ever going to happen. I was trying to survive, trying to change my life, and the last thing I was looking for was a man to fall in love with. Or so I thought. It was, of course, exactly what I was looking for.

My sexuality has always been very erratic. There are times when I couldn't be less interested in it and other times when I'm hardly interested in anything else. And when I'm into it, I use it the way other people use drugs or alcohol. I go on binges. I'm not into mean sex or group sex or props. The moment somebody steps out of the closet in a rubber suit, a bottle of baby oil, a whip, some flippers and a big grin, I'm out the door. I'm into OD sex, excessive sex, sex that is so high and instinct driven and good that I'm going to overindulge, I'm going to wallow in it, I'm going to get lewd, break the rules and go too far. I want to get millions of tokes over the line.

It becomes sex as blood sport for me, the one place on earth I can do only what I want when I want the way I want. I'm never kind. I'm never generous. I'm never charitable. I try not to hurt anyone's feelings, but neither do I feel I owe anyone anything. That's for me, only for me. If my taking is a gift to the other person, terrific, but what I really want is another taker like myself. To me, the best of all possible sexual worlds is two takers in bed with each other.

Which is exactly how it was with McGuane. The one-on-one combat was precisely the thing he liked best about it. And for the first time in my life, I met my match. I had a peer, a worthy opponent. I wanted the sport more than I wanted the blood; but when you play it that way, sometimes you draw blood. Most of the men I'd been involved with at that level liked the blood more than the sport, so I never considered them worthy opponents in the long run. But McGuane and I were evenly matched.

He was Captain Berserko. The greatest kick in the world for him was breaking the rules, whatever they were. Becky once said we were like twins, that if he had been born a woman he would have been me and if I had been a man I would have been him. We share all the same character flaws. We are both creatures of excess. If you can't do it to excess, why bother to do it at all? We both want everything our way every minute. We are both selfish. We are both megalomaniacal. And we were both consumed in a frenzy of terminal horniness.

The weeks I spent in Montana triggered off the most flagrant, scandalous, slatternly, offensive-to-the-general-public love affair two people can have. It was high and wonderful, and it was low, mean, and dirty and hurt as much as anything can. There was nothing peaceful or gentle about it. "I'm not looking for peace," I told him. "I'll have plenty of peace when they put me six feet under the ground."

I was prepared for it to end when I left Montana to start rehearsing *Cat*. "I don't want to live with you, McGuane," I told him as we said good-bye. "I don't even want to see you very much. I want to meet you in motel rooms a couple of times a year and go off on two-week binges with you."

But when I got to Connecticut, we began calling each other every night. I talked as much to Becky as I did to him. Two weeks later *Rancho Deluxe* finished shooting and he flew to Stratford to visit.

I had to go straight to rehearsal after I picked him up at the airport, and he wanted to come along to see what it was like. It turned out to be a particularly rough one, so I had some mixed feelings about his being there. When we finally broke for the day, I took him for a walk around the old cemetery behind the church where we rehearsed. I started to extenuate and rationalize the difficulties he had watched us trying to work out, but he cut me off and for the next three hours did a running monologue on everything he had seen. It was more than strokes. He gave me the gift of his curiosity, his enthusiasm, his respect.

I never before had the courage to think of myself as an artist, much less call myself one. I didn't have the arrogance of my dreams. But that afternoon McGuane made me feel that what I did mattered, that I wasn't just a cheap show-business floozy who was a shallow television actress.

"We are the artists of our generation, Elizabeth, not those esoteric, aesthetic people who sit around the universities. We're in the ballpark and we are the players—all of us, those who know it and those who don't. We're all part of the same community, and we all have something to give to each other."

He was the first person to make me believe I wasn't an outsider, the first to make it possible for me to begin to express my aspirations, arrogance, and conceit without shame. McGuane gave me my strut. It was a wonderful present.

The whole time he was there we carried on as outrageously and absurdly as two alleycats mating in full moon on the back-yard fence. We shouldn't have been on the planet much less Connecticut, which is still a place where a husband and wife can be hauled off to jail for engaging in one of the more popular sexual variations. McGuane egged me on, but he never had to twist my arm.

One day when I had the afternoon off we drove over to Milford to catch the matinee of *The Sting* at the local movie theater. We were the only two people in the place, and after we took our seats down front he turned to me and said, "Do you think we can smoke a joint?

Who'll know? There's nobody here but us, right?" We were giggling and laughing like fifteen-year-olds, when I suddenly realized he was all over me and about to go for the gusto.

I pulled myself together enough to say, "McGuane! McGuane, you can't do that. We cannot get laid in the movie theater in Milford, Connecticut, in the middle of the afternoon while watching *The Sting*." But he was big and strong and insistent. I thought it was more fun than anything I had ever done in my life.

Afterward, McGuane excused himself to go to the men's room. When he came back he leaned over and whispered in my ear.

"I have something to tell you."

"What is it?"

"We were operating on the assumption we were alone. Very slowly turn around and look at about the third row from the back."

"What will I see?"

"You will see two little old ladies in their sixties who look like they are perhaps schoolteachers. I would like for you to notice when you get up and walk back to the ladies' room how well lit we were by the light spill from the screen."

"McGuane!"

"That's right."

I walked up the aisle without looking to the right or the left. If there were two ladies there, I didn't want to see them. However, there were two ladies in the bathroom, and when they saw me walk in they bolted out the door.

We decided to catch the end of the movie some other time. As we got back into the car, McGuane began laughing maniacally.

"Can't you see it?" he cackled. "Do you know what the headlines in the *National Enquirer* would be if we'd gotten busted? 'Popcorn, Pussy and Pot! Star Blows Scribe at Milford Matinee!' "

That's how badly we behaved. We had no shame, no sense of decency. We outraged everyone. We were thrown out of public places because we weren't able to act right. We took terrible risks, making love in my dressing room and in the ladies' room of a restaurant while he held his back against the door to keep it closed. I loved every minute of it.

We were in the middle of a heat wave the day Tennessee Williams flew up to observe a rough run-through. The old church where we worked was stifling hot, but he appeared in his perfectly pressed white suit, white hat, and dark glasses and sat there with all the elegance and composure of a Southern gentleman savoring a balmy afternoon on a veranda shaded by bougainvilleas.

I could hear his laughter all the way through the performance. He seemed to be enjoying himself, but I was a nervous wreck. Tennessee Williams writes the language so well that he is one of the few playwrights whose every word should probably be spoken exactly as written, but I had taken it upon myself to change some of Maggie's lines around to make the pacing more comfortable.

When we came to the end, he stood up and thanked us and said he was flattered and grateful. He was especially pleased we had gone back to his original text rather than the version that had been done on Broadway. Much of the language in the Broadway production had been censored heavily, and Elia Kazan had insisted he rewrite the third act to give the play a more upbeat ending.

I waited until the other actors finished what they had to say to him. Then with great trepidation I went over and asked him if it was all right that I had tampered with his words.

He said, "Oh, darlin', however it was you were sayin' it, you say it that way. Everythin' you are doin' is wonderful. It's just wonderful."

I knew he was telling me that mainly because he didn't want to discuss it—he's a real artist, not somebody who talks it—but I wanted to throw my arms around him anyhow.

We had met briefly years before when Jimmy Farentino was doing *Night of the Iguana,* and I remembered how shy he was and how frightfully uncomfortable it made him to have to talk about his work or listen to praise. But I couldn't help myself. There was something I had to tell him.

Tennessee Williams is a man who has been maligned and ripped apart by jackals as only a great artist can be because a great artist is large and most people feel small. It makes them more secure if they can see an artist bleeding rather than standing strong. They can't wait to write him off. You see them at Sardi's after one of his plays opens making sucking noises with their mouths and wagging their heads while they wrap their claws around twelve martinis, just dying to count him dead and out.

And because Tennessee Williams is a real artist and not a corporation or an insurance salesman he is still vulnerable and frail and always has one foot firmly planted in madness. Sometimes he is drunk and sometimes he is out of control, but it is the ones who are never out of control who have cashed it in. Tennessee Williams still suffers, and when he suffers he suffers for every human being who has ever lived. He is living out his life for all of us. I thought it important to try to tell him some of that.

I took hold of both his hands and said, "You are a

great artist, and standing with you here I feel as though I am on hallowed ground."

He ducked his head in embarrassment.

"I know that it is embarrassing. It is as embarrassing for me to say as it is for you to hear. But somebody has to tell you that, just on the off chance not enough people do because they don't want to feel like the asshole I feel right now."

And at that he just hugged me.

He stayed around for the next few days, and one afternoon I picked him up in my car and took him for a ride around Connecticut. We dished more than we looked at the scenery. He has a heavy Southern accent with a little bit of a lisp, and I imitated it exactly, which made him understand me better. The play and the production were the last things he wanted to talk about. What he wanted to do was gossip.

McGuane and Becky had gotten quite close to him when they were his neighbors in Key West, and he was fascinated by what we were all up to. He wanted me to tell him every lurid detail, though he didn't at all approve of it. He's very much a Victorian gentleman in certain ways and thought we were being naughty.

Before he left, McGuane and I had a drink with him, and he told us, "I imagine that sex between a man and a woman is probably a very beautiful thing. But you have to understand it's somethin' that's beyond me. When I was still a very young boy, I was taken to a whore house for my initiation into manhood, and this woman made me look right between her legs. I don't know, all I could see was somethin' that looked like a dyin' orchid. Consequently I have never been comfortable either with orchids or women."

A couple of evenings later McGuane and I stopped by Michael Kahn's house to have our usual after-rehearsal bottle of gin together. When we walked in, we found the place filled with people who had come up for the opening of *Romeo and Juliet,* the other play being done at Stratford that summer. I was so into my own work I had forgotten all about it. I was just starting to settle in when a lisping voice behind me pulled my attention.

"Michael, why on earth are you reviving that tired old shoe of Tennessee's? I mean, Tennessee is only a second-rate playwright, and *Cat on a Hot Tin Roof,* God knows, is only a fourth-rate play."

My head snapped around in rage, and I saw a face full of embittered waste that belonged in a Visconti movie. The words leapt from my mouth.

"Sir, is it not the way of curs and mongrels always to chew on the tails of champions?"

The man backed away in horror, and I heard some viper tongues whispering in the next room.

Michael collapsed on the couch and doubled over in laughter.

"Well, sweetheart, you'll never get a good review in the New York *Post* again."

"Why not?"

"Why not? Because that was Martin Gottfried, the *Post* critic. That's why not."

I broke up and threw myself down next to him.

"But I *did* say 'sir.' "

Michael was right, of course. Gottfried got me for *Cat* —I think he said I was posing like a transvestite in what could only be my distorted idea of sexuality—and he's gotten me ever since. So much for critical objectivity and the pleasures and perils of hanging out with our critics.

Michael was as sensitive a director as any actress could hope for. Like all really good directors he fed the parts of me that were cooking and gave solace to the parts of me that weren't. He gave me the confidence I needed by making me feel beautiful and powerful and full of juice. But he also recognized I was on about something special.

We never sat down and talked about it, but he realized that to do the part right the main thing I had to do was get looser. It was more important for me to get rid of the emotional discipline and open up the floodgates than it was to make everyone secure by learning my lines and deciding exactly how I was going to play it. Every actor knows that for as much as you have to be in control to get there you also have to spend a lot of time out of control. Normally that makes the producers and director extremely nervous, so to do your job better and make them more money you have to sneak time out for that and try not to get caught at it.

Michael had never been an actor himself, but he understood all about that. When he started to do some intensive work with Keir Dullea and Fred Gwynne, two of the other principals, he gave me four days off to go on a total trash out with McGuane. He knew it was better for me and the play to use the time doing sex and getting loaded than for memorizing my lines.

McGuane and I packed a small suitcase, dressed up in our most outlandish drag, and got on the train for New York. We must have looked like creatures from Mars to the good commuters riding with us. I was wearing ostrich feathers, sequins on my eyes, and five-inch platform heels. McGuane had on a sateen Day-Glo cowboy shirt and flowers in his hair. As we pulled out of the station, he reached into his pocket and took out two psylocibin mushrooms, which we munched on as the suburbs of Connecticut sped past. Half an hour later the mushrooms hit, and we began laughing and thrashing about hysterically like the happy maniacs we were.

The conductor came through and announced that

the trains in front of us were all backed up, so instead of going to Grand Central Station we would have to get off at 125th Street in the middle of Harlem. It was ten o'clock on a Friday night when we were deposited on the sidewalk, and we just stood there giggling and reeling like two creatures from outer space down here on a bender.

They say God protects drunks and fools, and I guess He does. Three bad-looking bloods bopping down the street stopped in front of us to check us out. I managed to get myself together enough to say, "Man, we need a cab, bad," and they got us one. As we stumbled aboard, they broke up and waved to us, "Have fun, y'all!"

We spent the next two days and nights limoing from one end of Manhattan to the other, visiting everyone we knew and going everywhere we could think of. Our last day in town we went to Bendel's and bought a beautiful antique silver box for Becky, then over to F.A.O. Schwarz for toys for our kids, then on to the Russian Tea Room where we got deliciously high. As we sat there catching our breath for the first time in four days, something hit me and I began to laugh and cry at the same time.

"Know what, McGuane?" I said to him. "At this moment of my life, right here and now, I have everything I want exactly the way I want it. I have work that I love, that is challenging and thrilling and as good as it gets. There is a man I am madly in love with, and I have a relationship with him that is the only possible kind of relationship for me. I've managed to break the rules, and I seem to be getting away with it."

The world had always told me that you can't have it both ways. Either you're a nun and an artist or you're irresponsible and tarty and don't get to work. Everything— my mother, my life, my husband—had taught me that you can't have both a man and your work, yet something in me was always protesting, "No, I can, I can, I can." Even as life continued to teach me that you can't, I always secretly believed that I could have my cake and eat it too.

And what struck me as I sat there in the Russian Tea Room that afternoon was the realization that I *have* to have my cake and eat it too because if I don't have my cake I can't eat. And it hit me that the only reason I was able to get it the way I wanted it was because I had finally figured out what it is I wanted. And that the only way I figured that out was by getting everything I could and then ridding myself of all the stuff that wasn't me, that I didn't want, that didn't make me happy. The old process of elimination scam.

I had to get everything to know I didn't want everything. It took me thirty-five years, but I finally figured out exactly how I liked to live.

The next week McGuane went home to Becky in Montana, and I put all my energies back on Maggie, trying to penetrate further into the emotional realities of her character so I could play them out on stage.

I always have to know what the conflicts in a character are, the differences between the persona everyone sets up and sells to the world and what one is really feeling and thinking in one's deepest, darkest, most secret self. I try to find the two forces that are in conflict and then work them against each other toward the moment of explosion or implosion.

Maggie was a rush of rich things that way because what she feels and wants are so very different from what she says and does. The line I took on her was that because she has to get her huband Brick to make her pregnant before Big Daddy dies, she's facing a moment-by-moment countdown and fast running out of time. With every second that ticks past, her control over her persona is slipping further away from her. What she's really feeling is welling up in her like the fire in a volcano and she doesn't know how much longer the rock can hold in the fire.

To find those things in a character, you have to find them in yourself. And you can't find them objectively. You have to find them subjectively. You have to remember the analogous situations in your own life and try to recall precisely how they felt when you were going through them. And that's rarely simple because emotions are rarely simple.

If you're trying to find how to respond to being insulted, it's not enough to say, well, you get angry. It's more of a labyrinth than that, more of a riddle and a puzzle. In my case, if someone insults me, the first thing that happens is I doubt myself and tend to believe it, then I become guilty, and then I keep moving through all sorts of other emotional changes until I finally arrive at the anger. It's all a very circuitous route. A good actor won't go directly to the anger but will follow the path that leads him there because generally what you are angry at is less the insult itself than the interior trip the person who insulted you has forced you to take.

The object is to re-create the moment-to-moment, second-to-second reality of that trip so you can illuminate it to other people. And you have to be careful not to make your choices too soon. You can find something that works well enough, but there may be a lot you still haven't considered.

After spending the day rehearsing, I would go back to my place and have dinner with Christian and Christine, then get in bed and smoke a joint to relax my stream of consciousness and pull down the disciplines of my mind. All sorts of memories, metaphors, and analogies would start to come to me that I never would have found if I had gone looking for them.

If you willfully try to hunt them down, you'll never find them. It's like trying to pick up running water in your hand. You won't be able to hold it if you grab for it. You have to leave your hand loose and quite literally go with the flow.

I remembered my father when he remarried and thought his new wife's family was so fine that he wasn't quite sure I would do, how he humiliated me in front of my stepmother when I was visiting them as a kid: "Well, she's never been taught anything. That's why she doesn't know how to behave."

I remembered the first time I went to bed with a boy when I was still in high school and his coldness later in the face of all my virgin dreams and hopes, and how I felt I must have done something wrong for it to turn out like that.

I remembered Janis Joplin and how every song she sang, every gesture she made, everything she ever did in her short, magic life were all a begging for love.

I remembered George and how he was the Brick to my Maggie, how when it starts to go wrong for the man he will always blame it on the woman.

I used all of it.

And I hate to admit it, but most of all I used McGuane.

I didn't realize it then, but I had created in my life with McGuane exactly the kind of sexual relationship Maggie had with Brick before he cut it off. By the time we were through getting crazy together in Connecticut, I knew all about Maggie's ache, Maggie's strut, Maggie's gut, Maggie's crotch. I didn't have to imagine them. I was living them out every day.

I gave myself in my life exactly what I needed to

have on the stage, and I think probably any actor worth his salt does. (The comeback on that is, "Helen Hayes doesn't." Well, I'm sure that's true, but then who really knows about anyone?) To do the part right I had to get sex out of the closet and become sexually arrogant and exhibitionistic, and when I ran into McGuane I found the perfect partner for what I needed. The casting couldn't have been better.

I never sat down and consciously figured that out. When I met him on location I didn't say, "Ah ha, he's the one." It's not that cold. It's all from the visceral. In my work you have to listen to your animal in all things and go wherever it leads you. Your head set is what you have to get rid of. Logic, rationality, sense, coherence—none of those things will take you where you're trying to go. You cannot be manipulative because then you will be in control and you must not be in control. Large emotions by their very nature control you, so what you have to do is give yourself to them utterly. Go for the gusto. Dance where the music takes you.

I don't know whether or not McGuane realized what was happening. I suspect he did. He's too good an artist not to. Months later when I was bitching to Becky about him on the telephone, she said, "Well, perhaps you shouldn't overlook his contribution to you as an artist." At the time, I didn't understand what she meant, but I think that was probably a large part of what made our love affair so good. It made it constructive and positive and produced something I'm proud of, which is that peform-ance. I guess that's one I owe him.

By the end of rehearsal I had the sexual down. I could crawl that stage with passion. Sometimes an actor needs heavy inspiration to get certain licks, but once you've got them they become part of your gut. I didn't have to play the sex. I didn't have to work for it. I didn't even have to think about it. All I had to do was walk onto the stage and it was there. I physically throbbed with it.

Cat on a Hot Tin Roof is a magnificently built play for the actress doing Maggie. The entire first act is yours. It's practically an hour-long monologue. You're pretty much off for the second act when all the exposition and hard stuff has to get done, and then you come back in for the last act and get to tie it all up with one of the most beautiful speeches ever written in the English language:

"Oh, you weak people, you weak, beautiful people who give up with such grace. What you need is someone to take hold of you—gently, with love, and hand your life back to you, like something gold you let go of."

Does it get any better than that? I don't think so. To be able to say lines like that is a privilege and a trust.

And never was an actress given more of an opportunity to be a star as in that production. As the play opens, Maggie comes into her bedroom, takes off her dress, then sits down on the bed and changes her stockings while she dishes offstage to Brick. Michael Kahn found the largest, whitest bed anyone has ever seen, then placed it smack in the center of the stage and lit it with a bright white spot. No other production ever gave it that kind of prominence.

The first time we rehearsed with the bed he told me, "Okay, Elizabeth, I want you to sit right in the middle of that thing when you do the business with the stockings."

I said, "Jesus, Michael, shouldn't I do it sitting on the side? It's going to be awfully hard to take those stockings off, then put the new ones on and hitch them to my garter belt without being positively lewd."

"Nope, the middle of the bed, however you have to do it. And if you need any further justification, let us not forget that what you're out to do is not change your stockings but to get laid."

I think I milked everything possible out of putting on a pair of stockings. By the time we opened, I probably knew more about putting on stockings than anyone in the world.

When we opened at Stratford, some of the local reviewers quibbled with the performance because it wasn't like Elizabeth Taylor in the movie, but the word of mouth was so strong that after a few days it was impossible to get tickets. The New York *Times* and the other heavy press knew something was going on and began coming up to have a look at it. Mel Gussow wrote a four-column review in the *Times* that was like a love letter.

We were a hit, but no one had the money to take it anywhere, so when we got toward the end of the run we were expecting to pack it in. Then Roger Stevens appeared and decided that because of all the audience interest he would take a chance and bring it into New York for a six-week limited run.

This was before revivals were hits on Broadway, and there was hardly a cent for advertising or anything else. The poster had to be done on the cheap, so they used a rather provocative production shot of me bending over in my slip pulling up my stockings. We had to open cold at the ANTA Theatre, which is the elephant's burial ground, a place they bring shows that are supposed to be good for you which nobody really wants to see. When I walked into the theater for the first rehearsal, I said to myself, "Oh, my God, what are we doing? Is this set going to look shabby here? I mean, this isn't rep in Connecticut. This is Broadway."

At first I thought we would be sneaking into town, but then I began to sense from the waiters in the bars and the other people around Broadway that everyone was

164

waiting for us. More precisely, they were waiting for me. And that's never a comfortable feeling. It had gotten to be such an event at Stratford that there was very much of a show-me attitude about it in New York. It was, "Yeah, well, Ashley's okay, but a great actress? Come on. She's not even originating the role."

I was up against the hardest thing in my life. They were waiting to see me strut my stuff, so they could pass judgment on it, and in any situation where I have to be judged I am at my absolute worst. Count on it. I will go for the low every time.

I thought I could bring it off, but I knew I would have to do it under the only circumstances that might stop me from doing it. The one thing that would screw me up would be if I got self-conscious and scared and tight. What I had to do was get as loose as I possibly could in a situation that makes me as tight as I ever get.

The window of my dressing room faced out on the street, and as I sat there making up my face for opening night I could hear the people talking as they walked by into the theater. I reached into the bottom drawer of my dressing table and pulled out a joint of Thai stick a friend had given me. I looked at the joint. The joint looked at me. I turned to Ellen, my dresser, and asked her for an opinion.

"Ellen, the only thing I cannot be is nervous. Should I smoke that joint?"

She was her usual direct self.

"Well, I don't see why not. You do every other night."

I took four hits on it, then stubbed it out, and flipped on the tape cassette. The Rolling Stones' "Honky Tonk Woman" came blasting forth. That was all I ever listened to before I went on. The song was Maggie to a T, and I didn't have to hear anything else.

The stage manager called, "Places, please," and I lit up the joint again for three more quick hits and took my position backstage. As I waited for the house lights to dim, I kept telling myself, "The worst thing they can do to you is run you out of town, and you've been run out of town before. The worst thing you can do to yourself is blow it, and you've blown it before. So if you're going to blow it, let's blow it with excess rather than with careful, okay?"

The second I hit the stage all my fear evaporated.

I was so up for that gig I could have smoked ten Thai sticks and it wouldn't have made any difference. The rush of adrenalin was so strong I could actually hear it thumping through my veins: "Let me at 'em! I can't wait! I can't fucking wait!" It was like a thousand orgasms at once. There's nothing that can compare to it, and any actress who says there is either doesn't know what she's talking about or is lying to make her old man feel better.

The audience was as up for it as I was. The way the scene starts, Maggie comes blasting through the bedroom door and walks straight down front center stage to a floor-length mirror to look at the stain on her dress. Then playing it right into the mirror, she says the opening lines: "One of those no-neck monsters hit me with a hot buttered biscuit so I have t' change." But when I made my entrance, the applause was so huge that I had to hold my line until they were ready to settle down and listen. You can't just stand there and freeze, so I began turning around and checking my ass in the mirror, pretending to be so hung into it that I did a full circle. And from that moment on I knew I was home free. Maggie was there. She was there with me and in me, more than she'd ever been before.

It was like surfing. The surfer has to know the board and he has to know the water and he has to have the balance and the guts and the balls. He has to have a lot of things, but mainly he has to have the wave. There are dues you have to pay, chops you have to have, and licks you have to know, but if you have all those and you also get the wave and you hit it just right, it's like God hands you a magic bicycle and says, "Okay, kid, you get a free ride. Have fun! That's what it's for!"

But it had to do with more than ego.

I had a mission, and my mission was Tennessee Williams. My mission was to make the people hear the song.

And I was necessary. I was the medium through which the song gets sung.

My mission was to grab those people hard around the heart and say, "Hey, you with your piddling play here and your passable play there, now you listen to *this*! You're telling me that this man is a has-been and can't even get his plays produced? Okay, I'm going to stand in front of you and do nothing but talk for an hour, and I'm going to get you off like you havn't been gotten off since you can't remember when! And you know why? Because it's Tennessee Williams, that's why. And because I know how to do it. So don't bother yourself about whether it's any good or not or whether you like it. Just sit back and have a good time, and don't get in my way."

And they got it. They got it immediately. I could tell from the way they were laughing in the first two minutes.

The way I did Maggie some audiences would laugh in one place and some in another, depending on which aspect of the character they got. That's the joyous thing about playing a character as multiaspected as Maggie. But that night what cracked them up was Maggie's point of view, which was what I built her from and loved most about her.

And when you have an audience that gets your point

of view that quickly, you can't miss unless you start to lie or cheat, which was the very last things I was going to do with that play.

I couldn't do anything wrong that night. I have never felt so secure before or since, and I know I never will.

When the curtain came down there was a moment of silence like a massive intake of breath, then an explosion of cheers and applause different from anything I'd ever heard before. It was beyond opening-night overreaction and beyond an ego stroke. It was something shared.

It was you and them together breaking through the barrier that separates them as audience from you as performer, them as judges and you as the judged.

All of that was obliterated and ceased to be important in the face of the music, in the face of the song.

"Elizabeth Ashley left the New York stage slightly a decade ago as a lovely ingenue. She returns, still ravishingly beautiful, as an actress *assoluta*. Her Maggie the Cat is sensuous, wily, febrile, gallant, and scorchingly Southern."

—T. E. Kalem, *Time*

"Elizabeth Ashley . . . absent from the New York stage since *Barefoot in the Park* (1963) . . . is lithe and silkily strong, more *vaginal* than Barbara Bel Geddes in the first production, more feline than Elizabeth Taylor in the film."

—Stanley Kauffman, *The New Republic*

"Elizabeth Ashley was much praised for her Maggie in Connecticut, but even then she was sold short. Sensuous, withdrawn, composed and determined, Miss Ashley's Maggie vibrantly combines charm with grit. She can stand outside a conversation like a cobra, or flutter in like a bird. Splendid."

—Clive Barnes, New York Times

"Miss Ashley is hypnotic in every move: tumbling over and over on the floor like a puppy hurled from its master, swiftly finding her feet again to coil long white arms in invitation, taking a bow into her arms with the assurance of a Diana, spitting into her mascara as though beauty itself were contaminated. Her slow, small unvoiced "No" in response to Brick's asking if she'd prefer to live alone is a model of underplaying in a role that mainly demands fireworks."

—Walter Kerr, New York Times

"Elizabeth Ashley makes an incomparable Maggie/cat, afire with sexual frustration and determined to get her way not alone in respect to her husband's unfulfilled connubial obligations but also in respect to an inheritance that may soon be his. . . . Miss Ashley revels in Maggie's sensuality and calculating viperishness; she leaves us in no doubt that her Maggie could snatch from life any prize she deemed worthy of her."

—Brendan Gill, The New Yorker

"I have always considered Miss Ashley talented but rather chilling; here she absorbed me into herself, and made me see Maggie more from inside than from without. Hers is almost more of a juggling act than a performance, keeping grittiness and fragility, a sense of humor and an edge of desperation, sensual coquetry and sexless bitchiness —and God knows what else—flying around her head like so many complaisant Indian clubs. She is, if anything, too beautiful for the part, but performs with such astonishing,

such uncanny precision that not even her heady loveliness
distracts us from her acting. Miss this performance at your
soul's peril."

—John Simon, New York

Key West, 1975

9

When you are madly in love with someone—with the stress on "madly"—you are never more crazed than when you are forced to be apart. Absence does not make the heart grow fonder, but it sure heats up the blood.

While I was playing *Cat* in New York, McGuane was down in Key West preparing *92 in the Shade*. It was his first time out as a movie director. He'd only gotten the chance because Elliot Kastner, one of the last of the big-time hustler producers, had been so hot to get McGuane's screenplay for *The Missouri Breaks,* the Marlon Brando and Jack Nicholson movie, that he agreed to let him direct his own feature if he could bring it in for under a million dollars.

Actors will always work for nothing—they'll defer their salaries and take points in the picture—if they're in love with the person or the project, so McGuane was able to get Warren Oates and Peter Fonda for his leads and a wonderful supporting cast that included Burgess Meredith, Harry Dean Stanton, Joe Spinell, Sylvia Miles, and myself. I was due to go down for my part in early December, right after *Cat* finished its scheduled six-week run.

I missed McGuane terribly. Even with the huge success of *Cat* and everything that came with it, I couldn't stop thinking about him. We spoke on the phone every night, from the moment I came off stage at the top of the second act until I had to go back on again an hour later. McGuane had the timing down when I would be in my dressing room, and he and Becky usually called within five minutes after I got there.

The longer I was away from him the more I was in love with him, and the more I was in love with him the more strung out, miserable, and angry I became. All I wanted was to be with him, and I hated wanting it; I hated feeling it.

I didn't want those steely fingers squeezing the guts of my soul the way they do. I had been through all the love torments before when I was a kid, and they had turned me into a shaking, whimpering, desperate, manipulative jealous mess. I know what a junkie is, not from drugs but from love. That's the only thing I ever got strung out on. And here I was addicted again. It was turning me into a mewling seventeen-year-old, and I couldn't stand it.

McGuane was so preoccupied with his movie that he didn't notice what was happening at first. All the screws were going into him the way they do when you direct a film, and he was still a virgin, perhaps in the only way left. Everyone promises you everything at the start, but once you're out there you are on your own. Finally, he began to pick up that something wasn't quite right, and he jumped to the usual conclusion.

"Who did you see after the show last night? Where did you go? Are you screwing him?"

"No, man, I'm not."

"Really? Are you sure?"

He started replaying the same routine every night.

"Are you screwing *him*? Well, what about *him*?"

According to our rules, we weren't supposed to lay in on each other that way. But rules or no rules, territorialism was raising its ugly head the way I suppose it always does. We had been through it once before.

While I was still shooting *Rancho Deluxe* in Montana, Becky, McGuane, and I had long discussions about the ramifications of what we were doing. We agreed that we all love more than one person in our lives and don't necessarily love one person at a time. To be sure, to live with some kind of order, especially if one has children, one has to live sanely. Part of territorialism is primal and animal, and that part is right and has to be respected. But the other part is cultural conditioning and that, we agreed, is past its prime and probably does a lot more harm than good.

We decided that the three of us were going to be pioneers on the frontier of a Brave New World, guinea pigs in a Grand Experiment in breaking the rules and expanding the boundaries. We would follow our sexual instincts wherever they led us, tell each other the truth, and see where the lines actually were.

All well and good in theory, I suppose, but rather more complicated in practice.

The problems started with McGuane's second visit to Connecticut. This time, instead of waiting patiently at home, Becky had gone off to Los Angeles to spend a week with Warren Oates. Almost every man who met Becky fell in love with her and maybe she'd had one or two minor affairs in the fifteen years she and McGuane had been married, but this was the first time she had actually fallen in love with someone else.

McGuane could hardly tell her to stay put while he went flying off to Connecticut, but it was clear from the moment he stepped off the plane that he was having a lot of trouble dealing with it. He completely understood the contradictions and ironies, but the fact of Becky being with another man drove him up the wall.

Becky had said she'd call when she got to Warren's house, and McGuane spent the evening pacing in front of the telephone, waiting for it to ring. As the hours passed, he became more and more uptight, and began to turn into something else in front of my eyes, sort of like in a werewolf movie. By two in the morning he couldn't stand it another minute and lunged for the telephone.

"McGuane, what do you think you're doing?"

"I'm going to call her!"

I was furious. He was changing the rules on Becky, and that wasn't fair.

"You stick your finger in that dial and I'll cut it off! You leave her alone. You handle it and handle it by yourself. You can't have it both ways. You don't get to do that."

McGuane and I are very much alike in that when things don't go our way and we lose control of a situation, we both cop out on an "I-can't-cope!" We start to cry and sweat and shake and scream and break things. We become raving, froth-at-the-mouth maniacs. Becky and Warren, on the other hand, are just the opposite. They remain peaceful and calm, oil on the water.

Becky called the next morning, and McGuane almost had a breakdown on the phone. She wouldn't go into any details, but, yes, she actually had spent the night with Warren. Becky always mothered McGuane, and I could tell from the way he was carrying on that he was doing a terrific job of making her feel guilty and irresponsible.

I ran into the bedroom and picked up the extension to talk to her. She sounded miserable.

"Well, I don't know, Elizabeth. I guess I shouldn't have come out here. Thomas can't handle it."

I said, "Screw Thomas. What do you mean, 'Thomas can't handle it'? You do what you want and he'll just have to handle it."

Then Warren got on the phone. He thought we were all crazy and couldn't understand why Becky was putting up with any of it.

"Look, it's real simple. Becky and I love each other. You and McGuane love each other. Fine. Becky moves in with me. You move in with McGuane. Each of us has a civilized, sane relationship, and we all live happily ever after. What's the matter with that?"

I tried to lay out the ideology of the Grand Experiment.

"No, man, it's more important than that. The world has to change, and somebody has to try. And like the Zen Buddhists say, if you want to change the world, you have to start with yourself, with your own life."

Warren listened quietly for a minute, then summed up his response in a word.

"Bullshit."

By the time we got off the phone it was settled that Becky would stay the rest of the week with Warren as planned, then fly to Connecticut with her son and spend another week with McGuane and me.

The moment she got off the plane McGuane started in on her.

"Well, I hope you enjoyed your little vacation. And how is our good buddy Warren Oates?"

Becky smiled through it all as though she hadn't heard a word. But I couldn't let him get away with it.

"You dumbass! What's the matter with you? Is that any way to say hello to your wife?"

But then it was my turn to get territorial.

When we got back to the house we had to confront the inevitable decision about who would sleep where and with whom. Only one alternative seemed at all tolerable to me. Becky and McGuane would take the bedroom and I'd move out to the little guest house in the back.

McGuane didn't think much of the arrangement.

"No, no, we all have to be under the same roof."

Becky wasn't all that happy about it either. She didn't really want to be in bed with McGuane. She was in love

176

with Warren. She was in love with McGuane too, but not that way just then.

McGuane smiled optimistically and suggested yet another possibility. He would.

"Well, you know, maybe the answer is we should all sleep together."

Becky and I quickly discouraged any further pursuit of that particular thought.

"Whoa, McGuane," I told him. "You go too far. I have a long-standing prejudice against being in bed with more than one person at a time. So, please, don't even flirt with that idea."

Becky carried her suitcase into my bedroom, and I threw some things into a shopping bag and carried them out to the guest house. Our kids watched all the shuffling in silence. I saw their confusion, but didn't know what to do about it. I felt relieved when they ran outside to play.

I was too uptight to sleep and spent the entire night pacing back and forth thinking about what I had gotten myself into. If it hadn't been so painful it would have been funny. The man I loved was sleeping in my bedroom with my good friend his wife, and I couldn't stand it.

For all my talk about we'll explore it and we'll deal with it and for all my putdown of McGuane for not being able to handle it, I had to come face to face with the fact that I couldn't handle it myself. The snake had appeared in the Garden. As far as I was concerned, the Grand Experiment was over. I wanted out of the whole thing.

The next morning at breakfast McGuane and Becky were as strung out as I was. One more night of it was all any of us could take. The next day they got back on the plane and flew home to Montana.

I thought that was the end of it, then two days later Becky called and after much conversation we agreed to give it another try. Yes, the first round had been hard, but that wasn't any reason to throw in the towel.

It didn't get any easier.

One night about a week before I was due to go down to Key West for *92 in the Shade,* I got back to my dressing room at the top of the second act and the telephone rang as it always did, but this time it was Becky making the call. She seemed terribly upset about something but wouldn't tell me what it was. When she put McGuane on, he sounded even more peculiar. I could hear he wanted to tell me something but was having a lot of trouble getting to the point.

"Come on, man," I said to him. "What's the problem? What's bothering you? You sound all weirded out."

He took a deep breath, and the words came tumbling out.

"Okay, Elizabeth. What it is is that I've been having a scene with a girl down here. I've been screwing her. I've been screwing her all along. I've been screwing her all the time. I can't lie to you about it any more."

I had met the girl in question when McGuane and I had gone to California between the time *Cat* closed at Stratford and reopened in New York. McGuane had a lot of preproduction work to do in Los Angeles and had asked me to come out with him to help with the casting. I suggested some people, sat in on the interviews to help put the actors at ease, then gave him my readings about who I thought might work out best.

Among the actresses who came in for the ingenue was a young star-lette who had a certain quality I thought was quite good for the part. She said she had just crawled out of her sickbed with the flu and would be going straight home afterward, so I was somewhat surprised when we left the office at the end of the day and the secretary handed McGuane a note the girl had left for him written on a napkin from a bar around the corner. It said, "I think you're a genius. I love your book. I want to be in your movie. Please call me." But I didn't think anything much about it.

The big buzz that afternoon had been a six-foot-tall blonde iceberg of a model who came in for her ten minutes while I was in the bathroom. I had only heard the audio on her interview and couldn't wait for the day to be over so McGuane could fill me in on the visual. He told me what happened was that she sat down in a very business-like way, then promptly threw one leg over the arm of her chair and began to practice what in another day and age would have been called self-abuse. McGuane kept trying to talk to her about the part, but she just sat there smiling at him. He finally broke.

"Uh, look, it is rather difficult carrying on a conversation with you while you're doing that."

She smiled, matter-of-factly crossed her legs like Princess Grace, folded her hands neatly in her lap and said, "I just don't want to waste time."

I like to think of myself as tough and ballsy, but I have to admit I was impressed. I'd often wondered how those models get work as actresses because as pretty as they are, sooner or later they are going to have to do some of the talking part and there is only so much magic that can be worked on the dubbing stage.

For the first time in my life I began to believe some of those casting stories I'd been hearing for years. I always loved them but never bought them for a second. Guys brag a lot of ways. It's hard to be a guy. But mainly it made me feel old: "Boy, times have changed since I was going up for auditions."

Compared to that little theater piece, the mash note on the napkin was child's play, and I passed it off with a joke.

"Ah ha, McGuane, the young star-lettes are hot for your body. You're setting hearts aflutter all over town."

Now McGuane was telling me he had indeed called the star-lette and it had gone on from there, starting when I flew to New York to reopen *Cat* and left him alone in my house.

By the rules of the Grand Experiment it shouldn't have made any difference. McGuane shouldn't have been going through the guilt spasms that had him whimpering at the other end of the line. I shouldn't have felt like I had just been slammed in the gut with a ten ton sledge-hammer. We had never made those kinds of vows to each other. But there it was. Your emotions don't live by rules and conditions even when the rules and conditions are that there won't be any. The snake was back in the Garden.

Whenever I'm hurt and confused and scared, I get hard and cold as ice. It's a jive reaction, but it has its survival value. McGuane had finished his confession and was waiting for me to tell him something, anything. I could hear the armor clank down around my feelings as I said to him, "Well, sure. Okay. Fine. Catch you later."

I was sweating and shaking as I got myself together to go back on stage. I kept thinking to myself, "This is foolish. This is stupid. Our whole thing was that it didn't matter."

After the curtain came down, I had to race out of the theater to get to a late screening of *Rancho Deluxe* Frank Perry had arranged for me. When I ran back into my dressing room, Ellen handed me the telephone. McGuane was on the line again.

"McGuane, I can't talk to you now."

"You have to talk to me now."

"I can't. People are waiting for me. I have to change and get out of here."

I was struggling into my street clothes when the dressing-room door opened and a dozen visitors ambled in to say hi.

I snapped at Ellen, "Not now! Please get everyone out of here!"

The smiles faded from their faces, and as they backed out of the doorway I spotted a friend I hadn't seen in fifteen years. The only thing I could say to him was, "Man, I'm over the edge. Pretend you never saw me."

I knew I would have to take the rap on that one. Within three days, it would be all over town that I was bitchy and crazy and probably a drug addict.

When I got to the screening I was too spaced out to even see what was up on the screen. For two hours I sat there in the dark, brooding about McGuane and what I was going to do about him. Afterward, when Perry and the other people on the film wanted to know how I liked it, I had to bluff my way through.

My friend Mary sensed something was wrong and offered me a lift back to my apartment. All the way uptown she kept telling me how much she hated the picture and the way it treated women. Most of all she hated that I had played another small supporting role.

"I don't get it, Elizabeth. Why are you always doing those character parts, playing those bizarre women?"

My friends who do some other kind of work give me that one all the time, so I tried hard to hold on to my temper.

"Listen, man, I lost all the years when I could have made those kinds of strides in movies. The best I can hope for is a job with creative people in something that isn't

181

going to be too embarrassing. So please don't do that to my head. Don't ask why I'm not playing the lead sex-object girl. Come on! I'm thirty-five years old, for Christ's sake!"

When I got to the apartment my desk was littered with messages from McGuane. I reached for the phone and called him back. I knew what I had to tell him.

"Okay, now look, McGuane, what I really don't want to do is come down there."

He said, "That's why I lied to you. I knew you wouldn't want to come if I told you the truth. But I'm telling you now you are coming down here!"

"McGuane, you can get anybody—*anybody*!—to play that part. All it's going to do is hurt my show."

That was true. When I signed on for his movie I had expected *Cat* to close at the end of six weeks, but we were a big hit and the run had been extended into January. Just on the off chance something like that might happen I had a clause in my contract letting me out for the gig, but it was bound to hurt the show if I took off. We were heading into the weeks before Christmas when even the hottest hit in town has trouble selling tickets, and *Cat* was so expensive to run because of the large cast and crew that we practically had to continue selling out every night just to keep going.

McGuane wouldn't buy it.

"Ah, come on, that's bullshit. You don't want to come because of this other thing."

That was true too. The only reason I was doing the movie was to be with him. Now I didn't want to be with him. I wasn't about to get in some kind of cat fight with another woman to prove how much I loved him. The one thing I'll never do is compete for a man. I'm too full of predators and competitors in my own spirit to try to compete in the world. I'll lose every time.

McGuane kept pushing.

182

"I thought you didn't care. I thought you weren't territorial."

He was absolutely right, but I couldn't admit it.

We continued moving around in a circle until Becky got on the line.

"Elizabeth, you really do have to come. It's never been like this with us before, and this is no way for it to end."

I finally agreed that I would. A week later I steeled up the old gut and boarded the plane for Key West.

When I landed at the airport there was no one there. McGuane was supposed to pick me up, but he was late. "Okay," I told myself as I paced the airport waiting for him to show, "I'm here and I'm here alone."

From that moment on I knew that I had to abort. I had to scrape him out of myself. I loved him, but I had OD'd, gone too far, taken on more weight than I could carry. Now I had to clean up, and the only way to clean up is by not doing it any more. You don't play with it. You don't cut back. You don't make new rules about when you'll do it and when you won't. If you're truly serious about kicking a habit, you don't go near it and you don't hang around with the people who do.

By the time McGuane pulled up in the driveway, I was feeling so grim and desperate I was afraid to even say hello. He jumped out of the car and ran over to throw his arms around me, but the second he caught the look on my face he stopped short. My mother had always told me when I was a kid that I could communicate more meanness just by my expression than most people could by ranting and raving for an hour. I mumbled some kind of lame greeting while he tossed my bags into the back seat and we took off.

183

"Where are we headed?" I asked him.

"Back to the house. Becky has your room ready. We thought you'd stay with us."

"Absolutely not. I want to see Becky, but then I want to check into a motel."

McGuane shrugged his shoulders and focused his attention on the road. The only sound was the tapping of his fingers on the steering wheel. Then he cleared his throat and made another try at breaking through.

"Hey, Elizabeth, this whole thing is getting way out of hand. Don't you think we ought to talk about it?"

I shook my head and snapped on the radio to end the discussion. We drove the rest of the way without exchanging another word.

Becky was waiting on the front stoop when we pulled up to the house. Before McGuane could turn off the ignition, I was out of the car and hugging her hello. I spent the next two hours sticking close to her and my other buddies on the movie who had come by to see me. After a while the knot in my gut began to relax. Maybe it wouldn't be so terrible after all.

Becky was bringing me up to date as we ate lunch together in the kitchen. McGuane came in and said he wanted to talk to me about my shooting schedule for the week. We were going to have to work together, so I excused myself and followed him out to the back room he was using as his office. As soon as I came through the door he started to make a move on me, but I looked at him with such disdain that once again he stopped dead in his tracks.

"No, McGuane, it's all over. No more. That's it. I don't want you ever to lay a hand on me again. I mean it."

"Isn't there anything I can do?"

"Yes, take me to the motel."

I had done my own wardrobe for the movie, and

since McGuane was the director I had to have his approval. When we got to the motel I was all business as I unpacked the costumes and showed them to him.

"Okay, I've got this and I've got this and I've got this."

I was as cold and mean as an ice pick. That was the only way I could hold it together. McGuane, on the other hand, was still an open and vulnerable and caring human being who was trying to deal with a difficult situation.

As I held up the costumes for his inspection he kept saying, "I don't care. I don't care. I don't care." Finally he'd had enough and dismissed them with a wave of his hand.

"Fine. Terrific. Whatever. I don't give a shit about any of that right now. What I want to know is, is it really all over because I went to bed with somebody else?"

"You were screwing her in California?"

"Yes."

"While you were staying at my house?"

"Yes."

I couldn't help it. I was heading for one of the oldest and dreariest lines in the whole male-female drama, but I couldn't have put on the brakes even if I had wanted to.

"You mean you were fucking her *in my bed*?"

He threw up his arms in exasperation.

"*Yes! Yes, I was fucking her in your bed!* I don't believe any of this, Elizabeth! What are you being so goddamn precious about? A bed is a piece of furniture! A bed is a bed!"

I had committed to the premise. Now I had to play it out.

"McGuane, my house is the only thing on earth I own that is sacrosanct to me. It's my home, my space, a place of trust for me and my kid and my friends. You took some low-rent star-lette into my home, then have

185

the nerve to ask me what I'm being so precious about? You bastard! Every guy I know knows chippies, but they don't bring them into my home and into my bed! I think that stinks!"

McGuane's voice suddenly dropped an octave.

"Don't you talk about her like that."

That was all I needed to hear. The rage just erupted out of me. I couldn't hold it in another second.

I picked up an iron lamp from the table and hurled it at him so hard that after making wonderful contact with his head it kept on going right through the plate-glass window behind him then smashed down into the courtyard below. Our eyes met for an instant when we heard the crash. Neither of us could believe what just happened.

McGuane is the only man I've ever known who is as much up for the drama as I am. He fell to the floor, grabbed his head, and started to moan and roll back and forth.

I was terrified, as much by my own out-of-control insanity as by the blood trickling down the side of his head.

"Oh my God! Oh my God! Are you all right?"

I have to hand it to McGuane. When he's been thrown a scene, he knows how to play it.

He staggered back up on his feet, braced himself against the wall, and began wailing, "I've got to get out of here. I've got to get out of here. I've got to get out of here."

I asked him if he thought he could drive.

"I don't know. . . . My eyes, my eyes."

"What about your eyes?"

"I'm dizzy. I'm dizzy."

I steered him out to the car so I could drive him back to Becky, the mother of us all. The weight of what

I had done was beginning to sink in. But the rage still wasn't out completely, and there was a part of it that just wouldn't wash.

"McGuane, if you're faking . . . if you're faking, you son of a bitch, I'll kill you for sure!"

He seemed hurt at the very thought of it.

"What do you mean, faking? . . . I can't see. I can't see."

When we got back to the house Becky had someone take him off to the hospital for X-rays. Then she walked me around the back yard, reassuring me that it would be all right.

Before I had only hated McGuane. Now I hated myself. Never in my life have I felt like such a stupid, cheap, violent bitch. I had come to Key West that morning feeling betrayed and hurt and wimpy and sad because a man had been unfaithful to me, but I wasn't there three hours before I made sure I had committed an act of violence on him. On a scale of one to ten for bad, an act of violence is a ten while screwing around is maybe a four, so even if he was faking it a little, I was for sure the baddest kid.

That's always been a pattern in my life. Whatever the level is, I will lower myself to it immediately. I've never been able to walk away with dignity and grace, which is the one thing I've always wanted to do. And maybe McGuane really was seriously injured. And Christ, he had a movie to direct.

Becky saw what I was going through and tried to pull me out of it. With a terrible conspiratorial grin she said, "What are you beating on yourself for? If there was ever a man who had it coming, it was him. Hey, he's going to be fine."

We were still pacing the yard an hour later when

McGuane came back from the hospital. His information was a little sketchy.

"They said it was maybe a borderline concussion."

"What do you mean, *maybe* a *borderline* concussion?" I asked.

"I don't want to talk about it. I have a headache."

It was getting crazier by the minute. I wanted to get out of there and go back to New York. But that meant leaving the gig, and you just don't do that. I have never walked off a job in my life. There are no rules about how hard you play or how dirty you fight, and when things get rough it can be like a war. But you don't desert, you don't jump ship. The one rule is that no matter what's going on in your private life, your love life, your home life, if you are on the job and it gets down to one or the other, everything else goes on hold. If somebody dies, too bad, but you can't go to the funeral. As long as you can walk and talk and your kid is not in intensive care, you show up and do what you are supposed to do. Those are the only ethics there are.

I sat on the back steps with Becky and McGuane and told them what was going through my head.

"I feel like I can't stay here. I feel like I have to go away. But I don't know how to leave a gig either."

Becky said, "I think you have to stay. You'll hate yourself forever if you quit."

McGuane nodded his agreement.

I said, "Yeah, I know. You're right. Okay. But you've got to promise to stay away from me, McGuane. I can't deal with the work and this too. You've got to back off and let me be."

He promised that he would.

The next morning I drove out to the location to shoot my first scene. As I sat in the trailer putting on my makeup I hated myself so much for what had happened the day before that I began to cry. I felt ashamed, humiliated and, above all, wrong. A knock on the door signaled it was time to get it together, so I quickly repaired my face, climbed into my baby-doll-nightie drag and stepped into the sun.

Everyone on the picture had heard the story. While I waited for the shot to be set up, they kept coming over and saying, "Hey, I hear you nailed McGuane, got him in the head with a lamp."

People on a movie location can always use some action. Something has to keep them interested, and this was a hot one. Yet at the same time, without my saying a word, they understood that what I needed was to stay right on the work and for everything to be kept light and funny and fast, and they made sure that that's the way it was. When the star-lette graced us with an unscheduled appearance in a rumpled see-through coffee-stained nightgown that made it clear she had just crawled out of bed, then lurched over to McGuane and threw her body at him, they pried her loose and hustled her back to her motel before she knew what hit her.

I had to talk with McGuane about how he wanted the scene played, but I couldn't carry on a sane conversation with him. Each time I tried to ask him about the point of view or how he was going to frame it, my emotions came up and grabbed me by the throat. I loved him. I hated him. I wanted to talk to him. I couldn't stand talking to him. I was spinning through such changes that David Lean could not have dealt with me, much less McGuane on his first picture.

But as the morning went on I became more and more absorbed into the work and started to get pretty creative. It got even better when I saw that Peter Fonda, Warren Oates, and some of the other actors had shown up. They were all on hold and could have been off swimming. When you get right down to it, what is heartbreak? A mean, painful ego loss. So what do you need to feel better? You need to have your ego fed, and for an actress there is no bigger stroke than when your peers want to watch you strut your stuff. And when that happens, you can't just wimp your way through it. You have to come up with something.

"You want to see me work? Okay! Back off and I'll show you! I'll work for you!"

I got off so much that morning that by lunchtime I was feeling all right about McGuane. When he asked if we could have lunch I said, "Sure! Sure, we'll have lunch," then segued right into the standard actress-director patter. "What do you think about doing it this way? You want it a little more to the left? Fine, you got it."

We brought our sandwiches into the trailer, but the minute I was alone with him all my rage came out again. I wanted to kill him, strangle him, put my foot through his head. "Get out of here, McGuane," I snarled at him. "Just get out of here!" I was not what you would call a rational woman.

When we began shooting again, I refused to take direction from him at first, but by the end of the afternoon I was once again all light, high, fast, and snappy. It was purely psychotic behavior, but psychotic behavior that worked.

That's how the entire week went. A laugh a minute.

I wasn't due to leave until Monday, but the production manager knew how badly I wanted to get out and fixed it so I could finish up on Friday and catch the plane back to New York the next morning. Friday afternoon I was in my drum majorette costume, practicing twirling my baton while they lit the set, when McGuane came over with tears running down his face. McGuane and I are both dramatic, emotionally self-indulgent people, and we always cry when we hurt. We are the best criers in the world.

He sobbed, "All right, babe. I just need to know one thing before you go. . . . What's happened?"

I said, "Well, McGuane, what's happened is that we've broken up. We're not going steady any more. I've given you back your football sweater. Understand?"

God bless McGuane. He looked at me with eyes like strobe lights, then began laughing so hard his knees buckled under him and he collapsed on the ground. I started laughing, too, and all of a sudden everything fell into place. Not that it didn't still hurt, but a least we understood what the fuckup was.

We had tried to live in the fast lane, and it got us. It's hard to keep your heart in shape. It's only a muscle. I had thought my heart was the toughest, most calloused part of me, but it wasn't tough at all and couldn't take the pace. I had cracked.

Within eight months everybody cracked. McGuane and Becky would be divorced. McGuane would have gotten the star-lette pregnant and be living in London. Becky would be married to Peter Fonda. And Warren Oates would have fled for his life to New Mexico.

So much for Brave New World and the Grand Experiment.

The assistant director yelled that they needed another ten minutes to finish lighting the set.

McGuane waved back to him, then started to pull himself together.

191

"I'll tell you, Elizabeth," he said, "I feel as if I've lost my life. I sit here looking at you and I see my life and I know I'm losing it and can't do anything to stop it from going."

"I know, McGuane," I told him. "I feel the same way. The only thing that may keep me from falling completely over the edge is my work. I have to finish this gig and be on that plane tomorrow morning and get back to my show because that's the only handhold on survival I have."

The assistant director motioned they were ready to shoot.

I picked up my drum majorette's baton and gave it a spin. McGuane got back on his feet and dusted himself off. We walked over to the set holding hands, then took our places on opposite sides of the camera.

On the flight back to New York I brooded, "Okay, Elizabeth, it's time to hole up and go cold turkey, time to do what the Mafia in Brooklyn call 'going to the mattress.'"

I'd been there before. I knew how hard it was to kick the love habit. I'd been strung out on a man more than once, and it always did to me exactly what being strung out on smack does to a junkie. I got physically sick. I couldn't sleep or eat. I was wasted.

"All right," I said to myself, "here we go again. This is probably going to be worse than ever, but that's what you have to do."

To my astonishment, none of it ever happened.

I never had the sweats and shakes at four in the morning. I never had the terrible yearning and ache. I was never tempted to make the phone call. I didn't get that awful clench in my gut when I saw two lovers walking down the street with their arms around each other. I didn't hear a song on the radio and suddenly burst into tears.

I thought, "Well, what do you know, you've finally gotten older and wiser and stronger. You're not nearly as vulnerable as you like to think you are." But I didn't look at it too closely. I was so grateful to have escaped the agonies that I simply accepted it and let it go at that.

It wasn't until much, much later that I came to realize what it was actually all about.

I didn't have to go through the cold sweats and the bad shakes and the awful stringout in my life because that's what was happening up there on the stage every night I played *Cat*. Without being in any way conscious of it, I took all the deprivation I felt from McGuane and converted it into the deprivation Maggie felt when Brick stopped making love to her.

When McGuane and I were together and everything was so wonderful, that corresponded to how it used to be for Maggie and Brick before the trouble started between them. But that was just back story, what their relationship had been before the action of the play began. Now what the audience saw Maggie going through on stage was the same thing I was going through in my own life. I simply reconstructed it out of my own existence.

Now that I now had Maggie's deprivation, the one thing I didn't have before, my performance got better and the play got hotter.

When we had started rehearsing at Stratford, the first thing I had to work on was Maggie's sexuality; but once I found that, it became part of me and I didn't have to think about it any more. All I had to do was walk on stage and it was there.

But even after we opened, the part that was still

hard for me was that overlay of caged desperation when the sex is gone yet you can't get away from it because the man is still there. The way Williams wrote it, it's like being starved to death in a jail cell and going crazy from the smell of hot food that is just out of reach. Now I had that, and I could use it without even knowing that's what I was doing.

I suspect it will always be that way for me.

My life will always be dictated by my work. Whatever it is I need for my work I will somehow manage to find in my life. That's the gas that makes my engine go.

And I hope that never changes, because if I ever get so professional that I no longer have to do it in my life, it can only mean that the gigs have gotten too easy or I have gotten too slick.

It always has to be a balancing act.

There are times when I will do things that are dangerous, illegal, and ill-advised, but I can't wreck my life because then I won't be able to do my work. Yet I need the savage in me. It's my angel as much as it's my demon. I have had to curb my wildness from the moment I was born, but it didn't get killed. There are still parts of me that aren't remotely civilized, and I get to keep them as long as I know when to stick them in the closet. But as much as I shut them away, there are times when they have to come out.

That's why I'm an actress, I guess.

Because I'm a performer I can justify and sometimes sell the things about me that offend and shock the conventional world. I need to live life in the fast lane. I need to do things to excess. I need to go over the edge. I have an obligation to experience the things most people can't experience. The taboos. The things you're not supposed to know or do. That's part of my job. That's why I do it.

194

I would probably do it anyway, but if I did it without a reason it would destroy me. But because I am an actress there is a reason why I don't OD, why I know when to pull back. And that is what saves me.

New York, 1961

10

He began pounding on the door at seven in the morning, just like he did every rent day.

"Miss Ashley! Miss Ashley, I know you're in there. I want the rent and I want it now, or I call the collection agency!"

I stumbled out of bed and over to the dresser where I had folded the money away the night before. I opened the door just wide enough to thrust the sixty-five dollars through the crack. It came at him so hard he almost dropped his ledger book.

"There! There's your money, man, and it's for the very last time. I'm moving out of here tomorrow. You can find someone else to torture!"

I slammed the door hard and put on the coffee pot, then sat back down on the edge of the bed. I was exhausted, but I felt great.

I was twenty years old and living in a tenement in the Ukrainian ghetto on Twenty-sixth Street and York Avenue. It was a six-flight walkup with a bathtub in the kitchen, a john down the hall, and a sadist of a landlord whose biggest delight was harassing his tenants for the rent money the first dawn of every month.

No one in the building had the wherewithal to deny him his pleasure. If they did, they wouldn't have been living there. The other tenants were very old, poor Europeans who couldn't speak English and were so terrified of New York City they only left their apartments once or twice a week to bring home some food. I took it as long as I had to. I couldn't afford anything better and figured that the bullying came with the low rent, like the roaches and the broken windows that were never fixed.

But my luck had just changed. Two days before I had gotten a terrific part in a Broadway-bound comedy called *Take Her, She's Mine,* and now I could go for the extra twenty a month it would take to move to the studio apartment across the street. It was only one room, but it was clean and there was a partition between the bed and the chair. Best of all, it opened out on to a little bricked-over back yard that the *Times* real estate section called a garden, though nothing grew there.

The part was far and away the biggest score I had made since I came to New York a year and a half before. I had left acting school the beginning of my second year for an under-five-line part in a play by Dore Schary about the dangers of strontium-90, but it opened and closed in three weeks. The only person who liked it was Eleanor Roosevelt. I had also understudied the two female leads in a comedy by Sidney Sheldon called *Roman Candle,* and that turned out to be another disaster. It folded so fast I couldn't even collect unemployment and had to go back to waiting on tables and checking hats.

As it turned out, I was only out of work a few months, but when you're on the street like that, you never know how long it's going to last. Every turndown starts to seem like the ultimate rejection, and you have to face up to the possibility it may never get any better. At some point I began thinking, well, maybe I would have to go back home to Baton Rouge after all and find a secretarial job or someone to marry.

When Stark called me to audition for *Take Her, She's Mine,* I was understudying Barbara Bel Geddes and Betsy Von Furstenberg in *Mary, Mary.* The show was a big hit, so there was steady money for a change, but I still wasn't secure enough to think of myself as a real working actress. I was too afraid to. I didn't know yet if I would be allowed to stay.

There are lots of washouts and dropouts, lots of also-rans. You never know if you'll get to remain in the game. The only odds on your side are the emotional ones. And understudying doesn't quite count. The whole *All About Eve* thing with the understudy dying to go on for the star is just a myth. You've never been rehearsed, you're not properly prepared, and it would be a nightmare if you actually had to go out there and do it. I lived in terror that Bel Geddes or Von Furstenberg might miss a performance. Luckily, they never did.

I almost didn't get the part for *Take Her*. The day I was scheduled to read for George Abbott, Hal Prince, and Bobby Griffith I was flat on my back in the hospital with a kidney infection. I consoled myself with the thought, "Well, that's just one more turndown you'll be spared." But they couldn't find anyone they liked, so the morning the doctor let me out I went straight to their office and read for them there.

I was still weak and shaky and had to do it right off the top of my head because rehearsals were due to start in a couple of days and they still hadn't cast the part. After I had finished and they said the usual "Thank you very much," I figured that was that.

As I stood in the hall waiting for the elevator to take me back down to the street, I rationalized that I didn't make too much sense for the role anyhow. The character was a squeaky cute, utterly wholesome college girl, and I was hardly the type. I stood five feet six and weighed about ninety-five pounds and all my hair was cut off an inch from my head. I looked more like a boy than anything else. I was about as far from the All American Girl as you could get.

The very moment the elevator door opened, Hal Prince came up behind me and grabbed me by the arm. He was all smiles.

"We just want to tell you, you've got the job."

I stood there gaping like a fool while the passengers got on and off. I couldn't believe it. For whatever reasons, they had decided to cast against type. And it was a big, fat part, the ingenue lead in a play with Art Carney.

I found the energy to run the six blocks to MCA, then yelled and screamed my way through the oak-paneled maze that led to Stark's office. I literally boogied on the top of his desk while he negotiated the money with Hal Prince and worked out my release with the company manager of *Mary, Mary*.

I would be getting two hundred and twenty-five dollars a week, more than I had ever made in my life.

When I finally calmed down, I knew the first thing I had to do was move out of that roach hole and into the vacant apartment across the street. Stark advanced me the rent money, and I treated myself to a cab ride downtown to make sure I got there before someone beat me to it.

The next few weeks were like the beginning of a new life for me. I carried my suitcase and Che Guevara poster across Twenty-sixth Street, started rehearsals and costume fittings, and for the first time had my picture taken for a magazine. The photographer from *Show* set up his shot in my back yard and had me pose with a lovely little Siamese kitten a friend had given me as a celebration gift. Everything was turning out just terrific.

The fear had been gnawing away for over two months, but I knew for certain something was wrong when I went to the final costume fitting. The fitters rolled out the rack with the dozen dresses that had been sewn up for me to wear in the show, and as I tried on one after another I could tell none of them really fit. They were all just a little too tight around the waist and bust.

It took the designer forever to dictate the alterations. When she was finally done, I got back into my street clothes and headed straight for the pay phone to call my doctor.

"Look, I think I better see you."

"What's wrong?"

"I'm almost a week late. This will be the third period in a row I've missed."

He made an effort to sound reassuring, but he was obviously annoyed.

"I know, Miss Ashley. We've already talked about this, remember? I told you there's nothing to worry about. It's a perfectly normal response to the medicine I gave you for your kidney infection. Okay?"

"Doctor, please. My body's changing. I know it is. Two weeks ago I was measured for a rackful of dresses, and they're already too small. Won't you please give me the pregnancy test?"

I had asked for it before, but he said it was a waste of time and refused. I had been using a diaphragm, hadn't I? It was obviously the medicine. I was just being childish.

The prospect of being pregnant was too horrible to confront for very long, so I had listened to what he told me. He was a doctor, a real grownup, and must know what he was talking about.

But now I wasn't so sure. I kept him on the phone till he agreed to see me.

"Okay, okay. But please come over immediately. It's late and I have to get somewhere."

Two days later I called him during a break to find

out if he had the results of the test. He said he did and that I should come by right after rehearsal. That frightened me. Why didn't he just tell me everything was all right? But I tried to put it out of my mind so I could get the blocking right for the second act.

I ran out of the theater as soon as we were done and took a cab up to his office in the East Seventies. The nurse had already gone home, and he had to let me in himself. He took his place behind his desk, then smiled almost apologetically.

"Well, Miss Ashley, you're pregnant all right."

I was stunned. Even though I was certain I was, I still half hoped and believed I wasn't.

"But you told me—"

He shrugged philosophically and raised his palms upward to the heavens as if to say we were both victims of one of nature's little jokes and there was nothing much either of us could do about it.

"I was wrong. You are most definitely going to have a baby. Congratulations."

Congratulations? For what? I wasn't married and he knew it. Jimmy Farentino and I had been sleeping together, the way young actors and actor-ettes do, but it certainly didn't have anything to do with marriage. We had, in fact, broken up over a month before. What was he talking about? And, my God, what was I going to do?

The fear and panic had been sidetracked for a moment by my rage, but now they came back with a vengeance.

I broke down and started to sob.

"No, doctor. I don't have a husband. I don't even have a boyfriend. I'm in this by myself. What am I going to do? You've got to help me."

He looked at me like I had suddenly started to smell

bad. I felt the same way about myself. I was dirty and ashamed and guilty. I had always been taught that sex was something nasty and wicked, and that God would punish you if you did it before you were married. They were right. I had done it, and God *was* punishing me. That's what you get . . . that's what you get.

He scribbled down some words on a pad, then tore off the paper and handed it to me.

"Here. It's the address of a first-rate counseling service. They'll place the child with a good family if you decide not to keep it."

That wasn't what I meant at all. Didn't he understand that? If I had the baby, I could never bear to give it away. But how could I possibly have it? How could I take care of it? I could barely take care of myself. And even if Jimmy and I somehow did get back together, it would be the dumbest thing in the world to get married. We were just kids ourselves. Our lives were just beginning. I had just gotten a part in a play.

"Doctor, I'm saying I have to have an abortion. An *abortion*. Please. Please help me."

It was as though he had never heard the word before in his life. He refused even to talk about it.

That's how it was in 1961. Abortion was bad and dangerous and dirty and most of all against the law. You didn't read about it in magazines or hear it discussed on television talk shows.

He shrugged his shoulders again, looked at his watch, and rose up from his desk.

"I'm sorry, Miss Ashley. That's all I can do."

It was time for me to leave. But I didn't want to leave. I didn't know where else to go. But as he stood there smiling that fake adult smile, I knew there was nothing more to say. I would have to find some other way to deal with it.

203

I went back to the apartment and called Jimmy at the restaurant where he was tending bar.

"Jimmy, I've got to see you right away. I'm in trouble."

"Okay. All right. Take it easy, babe. I'll be with you just as soon as I can get someone to cover for me."

He did his best to sound confident and strong, but I could tell he was as frightened as I was.

By the time he rang my buzzer he had already hunted down a street buddy from Brooklyn who knew someone in the West Nineties who could do it. The friend had set up an appointment for the next afternoon. I would have to go there alone. Jimmy wasn't allowed to come with me.

It was three flights up in an old brownstone, but there was an M.D. sign on the door and the place looked like a real doctor's office. The nurse sat me down, pulled out a form from her desk, and matter-of-factly filled in the blanks as I answered her questions. Not a word was said about the abortion. The closest she came to it was the last item on the page.

"And who was it who referred you to the doctor?"

Jimmy had told me that's how it worked. The nurse would ask the question, and I was to answer "Charlotte DeMarco," whoever that was.

She wrote it down as if it had no more significance than the number of my health insurance policy.

The doctor was a plumpish European in his early sixties and wore a white coat. There was something warm and soothing about the way he shook my hand as he said hello. Whatever self-control I had left just crumbled away, and I began shaking and sobbing.

"Will you do it? Will you? You've got to help me."

He tried to calm me down.

"I'll do what I can, miss. But I have to examine you first."

He showed me into the next room, handed me a sheet, and told me to take off my clothes and lay down on the table. The professionalism of the routine made me feel it was going to be all right.

When he finished the examination, he washed his hands and said, "Yes, well, put your clothes back on and come sit down and talk to me."

He sounded too noncommittal. The terror began to well up again.

He was seated behind his desk when I came back into his office. He looked up with real sadness and shook his head slowly.

"It troubles me to tell you this, miss, but I'm afraid you're too far gone for the operation. It's only safe up to three months. You're already past that."

I was too stunned to say anything.

He began to turn disapproving.

"Why did you wait so long? Didn't you realize you weren't menstruating?"

I told him how the other doctor had reassured me I was missing my periods because of the medicine and had refused to give me the pregnancy test.

He shook his head again and kept repeating, "It's too late. It's simply too late."

"What am I going to do?"

"You can probably find someone else, but I can't advise against it too strongly. It would be extremely dangerous."

"Who can I find? Where can I go? Can you give me a name, a telephone number, something?"

He was still shaking his head as he walked me to the door.

I felt like the innocent victim of some monstrous crime, but deep down I knew there was no one to blame but myself. I had blown it again, just as I always did. To have scored that part and wound up pregnant was like the story of my life. Every time life had gotten good for me and it looked as if I might win, I made sure to screw it up.

When I was sixteen years old I blew ten years of ballet training by ramming my foot through a wall and breaking my toes. It seemed like an accident. I had lost control in the middle of a very fast triple piquet turn. But I don't think there are any accidents. And I was good. I was well on my way to becoming a professional dancer.

From the time I was a small child I'd heard my mother say that the one thing she wanted out of life was to be able to send me to college. She was a divorced woman who had to support a kid and her parents on a clerk-typist's salary, yet somehow she scrimped and saved the money to pay my tuition. But I couldn't even get it together enough to show up for classes. At the bio science exam at the end of the first semester I wrote my name on the paper, then whipped out a copy of *Peyton Place* and sat there reading it while the two hundred other kids took the test. I saved them the trouble of flunking me out by never coming back.

When I was eighteen I came to New York the way a young boy will run off and join the army because there's no place for him at home and nowhere else he can turn. Through the grace of God I wound up in acting school at the Neighborhood Playhouse, where for the first time in my life I found a refuge full of lost people just like myself. I waited on tables to pay my own way, and they told me I was talented and would be a good actress if I continued to work hard and hold it together. I knew it was my last chance and tried to do what they said. Less than two years later, when the other kids in my class were still pounding the sidewalks looking for work, I had scored the ingenue lead in a big Broadway play. Now this.

I was bad.

I was cheap.

I was nothing.

I would blow it every time.

I sat in the back of the bus, sobbing to myself like a crazy person. What was going to happen to me? There was no help anywhere, and I couldn't help myself. I had already tried douching for hours with soapy water, but it didn't do any good. Neither did scalding myself in a hot bath. If I had known how to do myself with a coat hanger, I would have tried that too.

Jimmy was waiting on the front stoop when I got back to the apartment. I blurted everything out before I even got the key in the door.

"It's no good, man. He won't do it. It's too late."

Jimmy was scared to death but kept trying to come up with something positive.

"I'll find Albert. He knows a lot of people."

There was so much coming down, that I couldn't handle and I had nowhere else to put it, so I put it on Jimmy.

"Sure, find Albert. But if you can't get me an abortionist, then you better get me some pills."

He stared at me hard.

"What do you mean, pills? What kind of pills?"

"*Those* kind of pills. I'd rather put myself away than have the baby. I mean it, man. The penance is just too heavy."

That hit him hard in his Catholic soul.

"Hey, wait a minute. You'd rather kill yourself than have my baby? You can't be serious."

"But I am. I don't want your fucking baby! Got it?"

He slumped down in the chair, put his head between his hands, and began to cry. I had hurt him and hurt him bad. I suppose that's what I was trying to do. That's the way that one goes, and it's so sad. When you're a kid in trouble and have your back to the wall, the one person who still cares about you is the very person you turn on.

He looked up and said, "All right, babe. Let's get married."

That wasn't it. It wouldn't have made any sense at all. Besides, he had waited too long.

"Please, Jimmy, spare me the noble gesture. It's not your style. If you want to do something for me, get me an abortionist and some money, or else get me the pills. That's all I want from you."

He reached over to take my hand. I pulled it away.

"Elizabeth, I want to help, but you won't let me reach you."

It was true. I couldn't take his love. There is no love left in the world when you get like that. I was back to being a small child, when I'd tell myself, "You're alone. You're all alone. You've got to handle this by yourself. You can't count on anybody. Get rid of them and lock the doors. Lock them all out."

I looked at Jimmy sitting there and flipped out at him. I had to flip out at somebody.

"Get out of here, man! Just get out of here! I don't ever want to see you again!"

When he was finally gone, I sat down on my bed and wept. The kitten jumped up on my lap and began to purr. I went to the icebox and poured it a saucer of milk, then got back into bed with my script and tried to study my lines.

The door buzzer woke me at three in the morning. It was Albert and his friend Diane, a six-foot blonde showgirl just off work from the Latin Quarter. She may not have looked much like an angel of mercy, but that's what she was.

Without speaking a word, she walked over to the bed and put her arms around me.

"Don't worry, hon. It's going to be all right."

All I could do was whimper, "It's too late. But I can't have the baby because I can't give it away and I can't keep it either."

She dismissed my despair with a wave of her hand.

"Albert, make a cup of tea. Trust me, hon. I know a guy. He's done me twice. It will be about five hundred dollars and you'll be okay. I'll take you there tomorrow."

Five hundred dollars? I had about three-fifty in the bank.

Albert came back with the teacup and pulled five one-hundred-bills from his jeans.

"Three are from Jimmy, and two are from me. Take it."

Diane arranged to meet me at the theater the next day after rehearsal. Then they left.

The abortionist lived in a basement apartment in the West Forties way over by the river. He was a large heavy-set man about sixty. No introductions were made. He had me wait in the front room while he took Diane in the back to negotiate the transaction. The only furniture in the room was an old office desk and a couple of over-stuffed chairs.

When he came back out he handed me a sheet and told me to undress in the bathroom so he could have a look at me. By the time I wrapped myself in the sheet, a large doctor's table had been wheeled into the room. It was the middle of summer and the place was swelteringly hot, but I was shivering.

He made his examination and said, "Well, this will take some time. You'll have to be here a couple of hours. Come back at two o'clock tomorrow. You'll be finished at five."

I felt the weight rise from my shoulders. He would do it.

"It will be six hundred dollars. I want it in cash. Please bring it with you."

I looked over at Diane. She shrugged. I said that I would.

"Do you have someone to take you home?"

That was the least of my worries.

"Oh, I can just get a cab."

He shook his head emphatically. I had missed the point. But if that's what he wanted to hear, that's what I would tell him.

"I'm sure I can get somebody."

I figured I'd be able to find a cab on Tenth Avenue. I couldn't call Jimmy. I had made it too ugly between us.

"Fine. But he must not come to the door. Arrange to have him pick you up at five o'clock on the corner of Forty-ninth Street and Ninth Avenue."

When I got home the kitten was retching under my bed. The next morning I dropped it off at the vet and withdrew some money from the bank. Then I called the stage manager and told him I would have to miss the next few days of rehearsal. My kidney infection had come back.

It was way too early, but I was on my way out of the house when the telephone rang.

"Elizabeth! It's David. David Faulkner!"

We hadn't spoken in over a year. He was an old boyfriend I'd lived with for a while. I had left him because he was too good and too nice. I had wanted to be out on the street. I wanted to hang out with the bad guys, the dangerous guys, the tough guys.

I broke down and told him everything.

He tried to talk me out of it, but I didn't want to hear it.

"David, please. I've already been through it. I've been to the legitimate guy who said he wouldn't do it and the careful guy who said he couldn't do it, and none of those people are doing me any good. This is my last shot, and I'm grateful to have it."

When he saw I was serious, he said he would pick me up after it was over. I gave him the street and the time, then left for my appointment.

As I walked down the four steps to his door I thought I saw a slight rustle behind the shade covering the front window. The door opened at my first knock. He was wearing an open-necked shirt with the sleeves rolled up and chino pants. A bath towel was tied around his waist like an apron. The examination table was set up next to the desk. The top of the desk was cleared of everything but a tray of medical instruments.

He counted the money, then went to the bathroom to wash his hands. He came back with a sheet and a bottle of aspirins. I'd assumed there would be some kind of anesthetic but didn't really care how much it would hurt. All I wanted was for him to do it, and if he couldn't do it, to kill me.

I only screamed once. He stopped and said very firmly, "You must not do that." I placed my hands on either side of my head and grabbed on hard to the end of the table. It helped when I threw my concentration on the exhaust fan revolving slowly in the window. When my hand jumped away, he said, "No!" and gave me a wad of gauze to put in my mouth.

I thought about a scene in an old war movie. The Nazi submarine had torpedoed the American ship, and William Bendix was badly injured in the explosion. The other survivors in the life boat got him drunk so they could cut off his leg without any anesthetic.

I banished the image from my mind.

"No. This is real. This time I'm not making it up. This is really me. I am really here. This is actually happening."

After it was over he said, "Here are two more aspirins. In five minutes I am going to get you up, and I want you to get dressed."

He handed me two Kotexes.

"Put these on. Do you have somebody meeting you?"

I assured him I did. He seemed relieved.

He disappeared into the back room but returned almost immediately.

"All right. It's time to get dressed."

He helped me off the table. I had bad contractions and couldn't straighten up. I shuffled into the bathroom bent over from the waist. He called after me, "No, no. You must walk straight. You have to walk straight."

"Yes, sir. I will walk straight."

Before I left, he made sure I had memorized his telephone number. He had me promise to call him at eleven o'clock that night.

All I was was grateful.

"Yes, sir. Thank you, sir. Thank you."

The two Kotexes hadn't quite done the job. I felt the wetness running down the inside of my leg as I walked toward Ninth Avenue. I prayed I could make it

212

to the right corner before it showed through my dress. Nobody must know.

David was waiting in his car and drove me home. He put me in bed, and rolled up some cushions and slid them under my knees. I lay there crying with release until I fell asleep.

I drifted in and out of consciousness until it was evening. Once when I awoke, David was sitting next to me with a container of chicken soup he had brought in from the corner deli. He made me drink it through a straw so I wouldn't have to sit up. It was the first time in weeks that I smiled.

"Oh, David. You are such a good Jewish boy."

By nine o'clock my entire body felt like your foot does when it goes to sleep. David took my temperature. It was just about a hundred, right on the borderline of a fever. But I was still bleeding and getting quite weak.

He said, "Enough is enough" and reached for the phone. "I'm going to call my family doctor."

He told her I was three and a half months pregnant and had had an abortion that afternoon. I tried to shoosh him. It wasn't safe to talk about those things on the telephone. She said she was calling for an ambulance immediately and would meet us at the hospital. My only concern was that I had to call the abortionist at eleven.

David rode with me in the back of the ambulance. They took me to a high-toned East Side hospital and wheeled me into the maternity ward. I watched the mothers nursing their new babies. I felt like a criminal and a freak.

The doctor looked like a younger Golda Meir. She said she was having me moved to a private room. I told her I didn't have the money. She said not to worry about it. When we wheeled past a policeman patrolling the corridor, she assured me she had already pulled my card. There would be no record of my having been there.

An obstetrician came into the room, and the two of them began to examine me. I watched the disgust and rage on his face as he lifted the sheet. I knew it wasn't directed at me. It was the anger a fine, fine doctor felt every time he saw something like that. I suspect he saw it quite a lot.

If I hadn't exactly been butchered, it was the next best thing.

The doctor said, "You'll be all right, but we have to clean you up. I'm going to give you something to put you to sleep."

I reached up for her arm.

"I have to make an important call at eleven o'clock."

She said, "You won't be awake then, but, yes, he must be called. David can phone him, but don't tell him his name. Don't ever say his name to anyone."

Somehow she seemed to know everything about it. I didn't find out until later that most upper-middle-class women usually went straight to the hospital after they left the abortionist. If they were very rich, they would go directly to the hospital for a "rest and test," and the whole thing would be taken care of there. That's how it worked if you had money.

She called David back into the room.

"David, call the number Elizabeth will give you. Tell the man she's perfectly all right but has checked into the hospital as a safety measure. Thank him and assure him everything is fine."

David was irate.

"If he'd done what he was supposed to do right, Elizabeth wouldn't be in here and—"

She stopped him in mid-sentence.

"No. He did the best he could. Now we will do the

rest. All you have to do is let him know he has nothing to worry about."

I woke up the next morning feeling weak and sad but mainly relieved. I was going to live. I was no longer pregnant. I'd be able to go back to the show.

I promised myself never to go to bed with a man again. I couldn't risk it. And I didn't want it, not with Jimmy or anyone else. Not that I blamed him for what happened. I only blamed myself.

I was a sinner and God had punished me. I was brought up to be a good Christian girl. They warned me that you weren't supposed to screw. If you did, the hand of God would descend on you. Your guts would be carved by a butcher. You would die. I hated the world that taught me that, but they were right.

I *had* screwed.

My guts *had* been carved by a butcher.

God *had* punished me.

I had learned my lesson.

Three days later I checked out of the hospital. The doctor came to say good-bye as I was getting dressed.

"You are fine, Elizabeth. You're perfectly healthy. You will be able to have children whenever you want. But until then, you must be more careful than ever about birth control."

"There is only one kind of birth control I'm ever going to use," I told her. "No man will ever lay a hand on me again."

I called the stage manager and said I'd be back at rehearsals tomorrow. On the way downtown I stopped off at the vet to pick up my kitten. He told me it had swallowed a piece of glass. He'd had to put it to sleep.

Everything died.

11

I went back to the show like a nun going into a convent.

Turning my back on the rest of the world and everyone in it, I threw myself totally into my work. Work was the only thing I could do, the only possible justification for my existence. I couldn't live a life of my own. I obviously couldn't fall in love. I obviously couldn't screw. I couldn't do any of that right, because look what happened.

Take Her, She's Mine was a lightweight commercial comedy about an All American Girl from a wealthy family who gets sent off to a college like Wellesley. George Abbott had staged it interestingly like a musical, with a lot of short vignettes that cut in and out very quickly, but it was essentially a string of recognition jokes calculated to get laughs from the theater party ladies who were its natural audience. The big joke was the father's anxiety about his daughter's virginity. It was all cute and innocent, like a situation comedy on television. Fortunately, there wasn't a shred of real sexuality in her character. I was so frigid and turned off I could never have played it if there had been.

I thought the play was stupid, but still more than I deserved. I was grateful to be alive. I was grateful to be working in a stupid play. I was grateful to be playing this stupid girl. I was grateful, grateful, grateful.

The script was originally about a husband and wife, but while we were out of town George Abbott had it rewritten to shift the focus on to the father and daughter. I was so self-involved I didn't even realize my part was being padded out and built up. I only knew I had more lines to learn every day.

You never really know what's going on when those things are happening. I'd always assumed it would be like in the movies where the producer sits you down and gets you prepared.

"Kid, this is your big chance. You're going out there a chorus girl but you're coming back a star."

But nobody told me anything. I'm sure the idea was to keep me busy working hard so I wouldn't have time to think about it and get nervous.

My sole concern was not to make any mistakes and do what I was supposed to do right so Mr. Abbott would be pleased. I loved him. I was terrified of him. I wanted his approval more than anything on earth. When the strokes didn't come, I became so confused and frightened that I called Stark from New Haven to tell him I might be blowing the gig.

"Stark, tell me the truth. Have you heard anything about a replacement?"

He just laughed.

"Well, don't you know that with George Abbott no news is good news? He never says good. He only says something if it's bad."

Looking back now, I realize how horrible it must have been for Phyllis Thaxter, the actress who played my mother, as her part was cut down and I was given more and more scenes with Art Carney. She was a sweet white-gloves-and-pearls lady who was in the middle of a painful and complicated divorce from James Aubrey, the so-called Smiling Cobra of CBS. Even at my level I had heard the gossip about his carryings-on with other women. I suppose that's why she came back to work. The play was her first acting job in a long time. But it never once occurred to me that she might be upset by what was happening to her in the show. She was a grownup. They never had any real problems.

It was years before I was capable of a clear thought, but I began to get some slight glimmer of understanding the night Art Carney visited me in my hotel room in New Haven.

I was trying to learn my lines for a new scene that had just been inserted that afternoon when he called me from a bar down the street.

"Hi, Elizabeth. It's Art. If you're not too busy, would you mind if I stopped by for a while?"

Without a second's hesitation I said, "Sure! By all means! Come on over!"

I didn't know him very well, but since he played my father in the show I'd gotten to think of him like sort of a real father. During the breaks he actually took the trouble to give me lessons about how to play comedy. "Play it real," he would tell me. "Don't ever wait for the laugh. And never play *to* it, because if the laugh doesn't come you'll be stuck out there by yourself looking like an idiot." It was all very casual, but he was the biggest star I'd ever seen up close and to have someone like that on my case just astonished me.

As soon as I put down the telephone I began to worry about whether I had done the right thing in inviting him up. In those days Carney still had a drinking problem and he sounded quite drunk. I'd always been terrified of heavy drinkers. I'd grown up in a world where people got out of control and violent when they had too much whiskey.

I'd never met a sweeter, more gentle man than Art Carney, but I remembered my relatives and the fathers of my friends—people I adored when they were sober—and how strange and scary they became when they started drinking. What was even scarier than the violence was the way they would never commit to the reality of being drunk. They didn't make sense any more but insisted they did. I never knew how to talk to them. My own hold on reality was too fragile.

What worried me most of all was what if Carney made a pass at me? How would I handle it? I knew I couldn't possibly deal with it without freaking out. Not now.

It was the farthest thing from his mind.

All he wanted was someone to talk to. He just didn't want to be alone. I didn't know it then, but he was at that point in his life where he was having to make the choice of do or die, and that one is as hard and lonely as it gets. Later on he made the right decision and he won, but back then he hadn't won yet.

Without even taking off his overcoat and hat, he sat down in this bleak room in the Taft Hotel, pulled a brown paper bag from his pocket, and began regaling me with stories and routines from the old days when he worked as an entertainer in Horace Heidt's band.

I sat there very still and listened, not quite believing what was happening. This fine artist, this famous star was in my hotel room, and he was wounded and he was afraid and he was lonesome and he was drunk.

When he finished the bottle he said, "I'm gonna lay down for just a minute," then passed out on one of the beds. He was still wearing his overcoat and hat. I put his hat on the dresser and rolled him to one side and then the other to get his overcoat off. While I was yanking at the bedspread so I could cover him up, he came to for just a moment, opened one eye and did his Norton character from *The Honeymooners*.

"Aw! Ah-*hah*! Uh-huh-*huh*!"

Art Carney is one of the funniest men in the world, and I burst out laughing. I covered him with his overcoat and the spread from the other bed, then said, "Goodnight,

Art" and turned out the light. I took my script into the bathroom and stayed there studying my lines until I had them down.

It was a peculiar evening, I suppose, but in some un-defined way I felt I had gotten close to him. We had made real human contact.

I woke up early just after dawn. Carney was sitting in the chair with his back to me, staring out the window into the grayness of the morning.

"Hiya, Art. Good morning."

He was so full of remorse he couldn't even turn his head around to look me in the face. He just kept re-peating, "I'm sorry. I'm sorry."

"Sorry? Sorry for what? Don't you remember? You did your routines from when you were with Horace Heidt and His Musical Knights. And when I tried to get the bed-spread out from under you, you did Norton for me."

He turned to face me. His sad, tired eyes welled up with tears.

"I'm sorry I imposed on you. And I'm sorry I made a fool of myself. Please forgive me."

I didn't get it. That beautiful, sensitive man sitting in the chair over there was apologizing to *me,* a creature who could hardly touch another human being, who had trouble even shaking hands?

I walked over and put my arms around him.

"Don't be sorry. Please don't ever say you're sorry to me. Not to me."

When I saw him at the rehearsal that afternoon, it was as if the whole thing never happened. He was up and wonderful and funny and supported everyone else with his strength. He was the Rock of Gibraltar.

I wasn't old enough or smart enough or experienced enough to know for sure, but I got a sense right then that nobody is the Rock of Gibraltar. I got just a little

221

hint of what it cost him every waking moment of his life to be that wonderful, funny, soft, vulnerable, sweet man. The price. I began to have a sense of the price. And that everybody pays. Everybody. I was a twenty-year-old kid who felt like she had paid with more than stigmata, and there was Art Carney still paying and paying and paying.

I didn't expect the play to run. As usual, the out-of-town critics wouldn't go on the line and commit themselves, but they clearly disliked what they saw more than they liked it. I thought we would open in New York and close immediately.

That was all right with me. I had been working long enough to go back on unemployment. I was even being paid a high enough salary to put in for the maximum money.

When the reviews were read at the opening night party at Sardi's, they weren't smasho boffo either. But since they weren't actually disastrous, everyone began congratulating themselves and screaming, "We're a hit! We're a hit!" George Abbott stood up and said very calmly, "Well, we're not a hit and we're not a flop. We'll just have to wait and see what happens at the box office."

Most of the critics thought the play was weak, but they loved Carney and they loved me. I was "the season's find," "vital and real," "attractive and talented," "exceptionally skilled and handsome," "a discovery headed toward the top," "a delight." I "belied the axiom that good looks and good acting don't go together."

It was an OD out of left field. I savored every word of it. I sat there in Sardi's in a dress given to me by Susan Stein, who got it from Jane Fonda, who got it from some Italian countess Henry Fonda had been married to. (Third hand stardust?) The photographers stood on top of the tables to take my picture. I ate it all up with a spoon.

Because of Carney the play sold out. I was not a star, but I was a star-lette, the hot little kid on Broadway. There's a new one every six months. It's like being prom queen.

Everybody wanted to take my picture. Everybody wanted to interview me. One afternoon I'd go running to *Vogue* for a photo session. The next day it would be over to *Mademoiselle* to shoot the cover. Journalists like Earl Wilson came around to ask me questions.

Where did I come from? Where did I study? How did I live? Did I always wear sweatshirts, jeans, and no makeup? Was I really a renegade? What did I think about premarital sex? American foreign policy? The Pope?

I didn't know what I thought. I had never thought about what I thought. When people I liked told me what they thought, well, I would think that too. What they were down on, I was down on. What they were for, I was for.

But no matter what I said, people listened. Whatever stupid platitudes and secondhand opinions fell out of my mouth were dutifully scribbled down and taped, and a week or a month later there they were in print.

I had scored.

I was on the map.

I had one foot firmly up on the ladder.

It was a whole new ballgame.

For the first time in my life, I was on the inside.

I was a success.

Everything in our world processes us to believe that success is the answer. If you are a success, you are good. You have the blessings of God. You are one with Jesus. All your wounds will be healed. All your problems solved. That's what it is. That's why it is.

As long as you don't have it, as long as you are just going for it, you have a direction. You have a purpose.

One that is condoned. And then when you get it, it feels great. It's like the first time you come. You never knew anything could be so good. Every itch gets scratched. Every stroke comes down. And you say, "Wow, I have done it. It is over. The devils and the demons have been defeated. I have won."

But then one day you look down at yourself and notice there are still some open sores. They are still running. There is still pain. There is still fear. Because the flip side of success is fear. And fear is the devil. And success is the devil's dope. And you start to go crazy.

One part of me loved it. Another part of me was intimidated, guilty, and scared. I felt like a counterfeit thousand-dollar bill. I wasn't a good actress and I knew it. It was just a matter of time before I would be found out. It couldn't possibly last. I knew I wasn't worthy. I hadn't suffered enough. I hadn't sacrificed anything. It had all been too easy.

After the show, the high rollers would come back-stage to my dressing room to congratulate me. They would tell me, "Darling, you were wonderful." They would leave me scripts and make me offers. I would listen and thank them.

Then when their limousines took them back to their East Side apartments, my friends from acting school would drift in. They were my peers, the people whose respect I wanted, the kids I felt comfortable with.

They didn't congratulate me. They didn't call me "darling." They didn't tell me I was wonderful.

"Boy! What a piece of shit! I don't know how you get up there and do that garbage."

I would shrug my shoulders and try to smile.

I didn't like the play myself. I didn't think I was any good either. I agreed it wasn't right I had scored while they were still having to scuffle. I appreciated what a bitter pill that was to swallow. I too remembered that I wasn't any great shakes in acting school. I understood they were all just as talented as me and maybe more so.

I would watch them look at me as if I had gone off and committed a crime. I had. I had sold out. I was in a slick, commercial play that represented everything we hated when we were at the Neighborhood Playhouse together.

"That stuff is the running sore of the theater," we would tell each other. "We'll just never do those kinds of jobs. We'd rather starve first."

We would also go to see great actresses like Geraldine Page, Kim Stanley, and Julie Harris and come out of the theater sniggering, "Oh, they were indicating all over the place." God forbid one of them went to California to make a movie or, horror of horrors, actually did something on television. "Well, we always knew they were just cheap shit."

It was the easy, defensive conceit of the beginner. Beginners are the most arrogant and unforgiving people in the world because they have done nothing and know nothing, and I was one of them.

That's such an affront to me now. If I now had met me then, I would have kicked me in the ass and told me I didn't deserve to be on a stage if I didn't value and understand where I was. Well, I didn't.

I missed the absurdity of kids living on unemployment and acting for free in basements who hold forth about selling out. But I did see that behind that there is an ethic and it's not a bad one, even if it's more aspired to than practiced.

Part of me felt that if I had any integrity I would be down there Off Broadway in my black leotards doing raging, boring avant-garde theater like the rest of them.

Yet another part of me suspected that was bullshit.

225

My mother always told me you had to work to support yourself and that takes priority over everything else. The worker in me believed that. It believes it to this day. If I only did things I respected and loved and thought were important, I would have done maybe four jobs in the past ten years. That's no way to pay the rent. But I wasn't all that certain about it then. I wasn't all that certain about anything. They were probably right. I was probably wrong.

Before they got up to leave, they would finish trashing the show.

"*Art Carney?* From *The Honeymooners?* Jesus, he really does indicate. It must be terrible to work with him."

Terrible? It was the highest experience of my life.

I would shrug my shoulders again and say nothing.

"And *George Abbott?* Come on! I mean, you can't do any *acting* with *George Abbott.* He just gives you line readings and tells you to do takes."

That couldn't have been less true. George Abbott never gave you line readings. He wouldn't allow you to do takes. More than any other director in the theater, he always stressed that you had to work for what is real.

I would say nothing again and thank them for coming.

I thought I could make up for it by finding them jobs. I'd call and say, "They're casting this new show. You're right for the part. Go up for it. I know the casting director." It was the worst possible thing to do. After a while they stopped coming around, and we drifted even farther apart.

Still and all, there had to be something more real than eight shows a week of the All American Girl. I wanted so badly to do something I could take pride in. But I didn't know how to find it.

I thought I made my connection when I went to a party in the Village and found myself sitting next to a young Off Broadway actor. He wasn't bad-looking and he wore tight pants, which would always get my attention. But I wasn't looking for a boyfriend. What interested me was that he worked with a group called the Living Theater.

The Living Theater was a truly important renegade theater company of the early sixties. It was started by Julian Beck and his wife, Judith Malina, as a kind of radical artistic commune. The actor told me how everyone in the company had pooled their pennies, then begged, borrowed, and stole the rest they needed to rent this old industrial loft on Sixth Avenue and Fourteenth Street. Then they all rolled up their sleeves and made it into a theater with their own hands.

"And the night we finished," he said, "I stood on the stage and could see five places where I had fitted the boards together myself."

It sounded like everything I wanted to be part of.

I took to going down there on my nights off to watch them work. They were doing a William Carlos Williams play called *Many Loves*. I must have seen it ten times. Afterward, I would go backstage to say hello to my friend and chat for a few minutes. While I waited for him to finish dressing, I tried to get into conversations with the other people in the company who were hanging around. But they never seemed to want to know me. They were always kind of cold and hostile. That was the Off Broadway style those days, so I told myself not to take it personally.

One night when I went backstage my friend was standing with a group of other actors. As soon as they spotted me, they began to giggle and laugh. He laughed

227

along with them and went on with his conversation. I was sure they were talking about me.

"What was that all about?" I asked when he finally came over.

He flashed a mean, ironic smile.

"Do you know what they call you backstage here?"

"No. What do they call me?"

"Miss Subways."

Miss Subways was the winner of a scuzzy beauty contest who got to have her picture up in the subway cars in New York City for a couple of months. They were saying I was cheap and shallow and stupid. It made me feel even lower than when I saw myself called "kooky" in the newspapers. That was the media's favorite word for me. I winced every time I read it.

"Miss Subways, huh?"

"Yeah."

"Okay, man. I'll see you."

I turned on my heel and never went back.

About the same time, plans were announced for the new theater in the Lincoln Center arts complex. The company of actors was to be directed by Elia Kazan. At that time Kazan and the Actors Studio symbolized everything good theater was all about. Any actor would gladly have cut off one arm and an ear to work for him.

I begged Stark to call his office.

"Oh, Stark, please. I want to be part of that. I'll paint scenery. I'll be an apprentice. However they work it— I'll do anything."

Stark had trouble getting through to Terry Faye, Kazan's casting director, but I stayed on him and called him every afternoon.

"Have you talked to her yet? Have you talked to her? Can I audition?"

Finally he managed to speak to her.

"Well, Elizabeth, Terry Faye says Kazan isn't interested in seeing anyone he doesn't know. He only wants to work with people he already knows."

"But that isn't fair!"

"Yes, well, that's what she said."

I realized I was probably being paranoid. They probably already knew who they wanted. They probably didn't have the time or interest to talk to everyone who came knocking on their door. Yet it still seemed to confirm the judgment that I had sold out. There was a real line drawn then between serious actors with artistic aspirations and what were derisively called "musical comedy people." I knew which side of the line I was on.

I went back to the high rollers and "Darling, you were wonderful." Joan Crawford and Ruth Gordon sent me fan letters, and I taped them to the mirror of my dressing table. People like Lucille Ball came backstage to visit me.

But that wasn't it either. I knew enough to know that Lucille Ball is a remarkable person. She was perhaps the first woman to run her own production company. But when she said to me, "I'd really like to talk to you about television after you finish the play. I think you'd be wonderful," I answered, "Oh, I would *never* do a television series!" The words just fell out of my mouth. Only when I thought about it later did I realize how insufferably snotty they were. *I* said *that* to *Lucille Ball?* My God!

I didn't really want to be on the inside. They were grownups. They wore coats and ties. They intimidated me. I was uncomfortable at their uptown cocktail and dinner parties. I wasn't any good at small talk. I never knew what to say or do. I was just a kid from south Louisiana. I was brought up to have good manners and knew how to behave in polite society, but the social rituals of the sophisticated Upper East Side New York world were quite beyond me. I didn't have the right clothes. I would make a fool of myself. The strap on my slip would fall. The heel on my shoe would break. I would spill something down my front.

Besides, they weren't inviting me because they really wanted me there. It was only because I was hot and my name was in the newspapers. They didn't even know me.

The first time I was invited, Stark forwarded the invitation from his office and I didn't know what to make of it. Who was this woman? Why was she asking me into her home?

"Her family owns Bergdorf Goodman," Stark explained. "She is one of the great patrons of the Metropolitan Opera. A very elegant lady."

I thought I would take a pass.

"I don't know those people, Stark. What's the point? And I don't really have the time. I've got to do three interviews the next day."

"You will be invited to a lot of places where you don't know the people. You are getting to be a recognized young actress, and they want to meet you. It's the world of arts and letters, my dear."

We both laughed.

"Oh, go ahead," he said. "You'll have a good time. Just take a bath and be sure to wear a dress."

There were only two dresses in my closet. I had bought them both on sale at Filene's basement in Boston the year before when I was on the road as an understudy. I pulled out the red wool one that might get me by, but the moths had gotten there first. I darned it up and hoped no one would notice.

It was winter, but my only coat was an old army surplus trenchcoat that was two sizes too big and hung down to my ankles. I left it in my dressing room and almost froze getting the cab.

The driver took me to a townhouse in the East Seventies. The front door was opened by a uniformed maid in a ruffled cap and apron.

"Good evening, miss. May I take your coat?"

As cold as it was, my palms began to sweat.

"Uh, I don't have one. You see—"

I was about to launch into some elaborate fabrication when the hostess appeared and introduced herself. She took me by the arm and led me into the living room. Stark was right. She was a very elegant lady. And like all truly elegant people, she knew how to put someone immediately at ease. I almost stopped worrying that they would see I wasn't dressed right.

One butler announced that dinner was served. Two others opened the doors to the dining room.

I never saw anything so beautiful. The dining table was about twenty-five feet long and covered with an Irish linen tablecloth, vases of fresh flowers, and more crystal and silver than you could find in the whole of Tiffany's. The room was lit by hundreds of small candles that flickered from sconces on the walls.

I found my place card and sat down next to a bass baritone from the Metropolitan Opera. Rudolf Bing was seated across from me. There were about twenty guests in all. Their names sounded vaguely familiar, but I wasn't sure who they were.

The maids carried in the first course and placed it on the serving table. The six butlers took it from the serving table and brought it to the guests. It was some kind of cold yellow soup in a large flat bowl that rested in another bowl filled with ice, which was set on a plate. I tasted it cautiously. These kind of people sometimes ate

231

peculiar things, and I had never had cold soup before. It was delicious.

When I got toward the end, I slowed down so I could see what to do with the spoon. My mother had taught me to put it on the side of the plate when you're finished, but there didn't seem to be enough room. Everyone left theirs in the bowl. I did the same and made a mental note. Okay, you put the spoon *on the side* when it's a little high bowl, but you leave it *in* the bowl when it's flat and wide.

By the time the butler cleared it away, I had unwound enough to realize how hungry I was. Most of the others had hardly touched their soup, but I had just gotten off work and, hell, man, I was famished. I was ready to tear into the next course. I didn't get fed like this every day. My dinner usually came from the Puerto Rican deli on the corner.

The maids carried out something that looked like ice cream. It was getting curiouser and curiouser. Twenty guests all dressed up, five hundred candles, fresh flowers, cut crystal and bone china, and that's it—cold soup and ice cream?

What it was was sherbet to clear your palate for the next course. That was another new one on me, but I sat there and watched what everyone else did, and when they ate theirs I ate mine.

Then the maids brought out the beef Wellington. I had enough restraint not to say, "Boy oh boy, roast pie!"

As dinner unfolded, the people at the table asked me questions about myself and the show. I told them about Art Carney and George Abbott and some funny stories on myself. I was aware enough to know that as long as you keep it humorous and light and don't pretend to be something you aren't, most people will probably like you. When the bass baritone asked, "What sort of parts would you like to do next?" I answered, "All I really want is to be in

plays where I get to wear dresses like this tablecloth."
Everyone laughed.

Before I went to bed I wrote a long letter to my
mother. I told her every detail about the evening, from the
maids in the ruffles to the cold curry soup to the fresh
strawberries dipped in chocolate that were passed around
after the first dessert was cleared away. The one thing I
left out was how peculiar and out of place I really felt. I
never gave my mother the down side of any of it. I wanted
her to be proud of me. I wanted her to enjoy my success.
I wanted her to know I could handle it.

I suppose there was also a vengeance in it.

You see, Mom? I can have it exactly the way I want
it. Life isn't a hard, endless struggle. I don't have to grow
up. I don't have to play by the rules. I don't have to do
my homework. See? They were all wrong about me. I
haven't ended up on the garbage pile. I am not a washout.
I'm not shallow. I'm not stupid.

The irony that that's precisely what I did feel like
did not escape me entirely. But as long as you are successful you can tell grownups anything. Even your mother.
And they will buy it.

Correction. There was one place where you couldn't
get away with it.

When you start to become successful, the first thing
you think is, "Hooray, I will never have to take any shit
again. Not from anyone." But, of course, that's when the
shit really begins.

The subliminal message comes through loud and clear.

"Okay, kid, you got lucky and scored. But now you
have to earn that luck, or we'll take it away from you.
Remember, there are plenty more where you came from.
You're a dime a dozen, and we can throw you back on

the garbage heap like *that*. So if you want to hang on to it, you just do what we tell you."

What they told me to do was publicize the show. Every few days the publicist would appear in my dressing room with another list of appointments.

"All right, Elizabeth, tomorrow morning at eleven you have to do this interview here. Then you meet so-and-so for lunch at twelve-thirty. Then at four it's a radio show over there."

At first I loved it. I more than loved it. I wallowed in it. I didn't realize how excessive the praise and attention could be. But then I began to notice how my entire life was being taken up by it. All my time was spoken for. I was running every second. I didn't have a minute to myself. And what little time I did have wasn't really mine. I was supposed to be home sleeping so I could get up the next morning and do it again.

It was neverending. Somebody always owned a piece of me. Someone could always claim my time. Everybody had a priority above mine about my life, my head, my heart, my everything. And I began to sense that all I was was a commodity, a piece of merchandise, a potential money-maker.

That started to become clear after I won the Tony Award for best supporting actress. I loved it when the photographers snapped away as I stood there holding what looked for all the world like a silver ice tea coaster while making my little speech. "Well, George Abbott's done it again." And I lapped it up when everyone laughed and applauded.

Then the next morning at Stark's office I listened in on the extension as he asked the producer for a raise.

"Well, I'm not sure we want to do that, Stark. It's not in the contract. But what we can do is put her name above the title. Give her star billing. Okay?"

234

Stark wouldn't buy it.

"Absolutely not. No star billing. Once you go above the title, you can't come back down. What we'll take is a raise, please."

I had been making about two and a quarter a week. I think they came up with another fifty dollars.

So then I had a little vision about how the game works. And it was no longer a matter of desperation and survival and fantasies and dreams. It was just a shill game now. It was all carnival barkers and hustlers and con men. And that will really trash you.

But I still didn't dare say anything. I had gotten my little bit of success, and now I had to nail it down. You can't afford to say no. You can't afford to be unavailable. The moment I indicated I would rather not do the interview or pose for the picture, it was made clear that I was behaving like a bad child, being selfish, irresponsible, unprofessional. They let me know anyone else would be grateful to be where I was.

I believed them and tried to do what they told me. But as the months went by I became more and more tired and more and more rushed, and I started to get irritable. And the irritation escalated into anger. And the anger modulated into hysteria. But I kept on racing. I raced to get myself together to look good. I raced to be where I was supposed to be on time. And I became terrified that I wouldn't do it right, that I wouldn't get to ten appointments in forty-eight hours. And I knew if I didn't get there, I would incur their wrath and disapproval and they would throw me away and get another one where I came from. I'd blow it just like I always blew everything good in my life.

And as much as I tried, I just couldn't seem to get it to add up. There I was. I had made it. I had what I wanted. I was supposed to be happy. But somehow the whole thing turned into a nightmare. I was even more afraid and insecure than when I had nothing.

There was no get-off anywhere, not even when I got back with Jimmy. I had longed for him so badly that I couldn't keep away from him, and after the play opened we moved in together. A few months later we were even married.

But the abortion had frightened me so that I was still terrified of sex. I didn't want to go back on the table. I figured I wouldn't be given a second chance. Whenever Jimmy made a move in that direction, I turned on him. And I was so busy running here and there that I was hardly ever around.

It was humiliating for him. He was a macho Italian street guy a couple of years older than me who was working hard to be an actor, and here I was a big hit in a play with Art Carney. He didn't have a dime. Whatever money we had, I made. I had a career going. He had a walk-on in a Broadway show. It all took its toll. How could it not?

If you are a young person who is pretty shaky to begin with and you get put through that kind of success trip, it's a miracle if you survive even reasonably intact. What you become is an eight-car crackup on the freeway. A grenade that has had its pin pulled. A time bomb about to explode.

(Remember Freddie Prinze?)

I began to turn into an absolute horror.

I had lots and lots of rage, and it came out everywhere about everything. I became quite temperamental. I yelled and screamed and cried. I took to throwing tantrums in my dressing room. I found out later they were the running joke of the company. Six of the actors playing college kids shared a dressing room right above mine and rigged the air vent so they could get a good seat. "There she goes," they would say as they called in their friends for a listen. "It's Bessie Von Bitch again."

The longer the show ran, the more out of control I became. It got so bad one evening that Phyllis Thaxter burst into my dressing room, seized me by the shoulders and shook me hard while she yelled over and over again, "Stop it! Stop it! Stop it! Stop it!" There was never a more gentle woman, but she saw I was a raging, neurotic child that couldn't stop itself, so someone had to do it for me.

*

It all came to a head the week before I left the play.

Take Her, She's Mine had been running on Broadway for well over a year, and it was now time to go out on the road. Joanna Pettet, my understudy, would be taking over my role. I already had my ticket for California and a contract for *Carpetbaggers,* but there were still four more performances before the show left town.

I had about a dozen costume changes that had to be made very fast right in the wings. When I came out in my first change that night I felt the waistline of my dress down around my hips. I assumed it had ripped in the back. You can't look down when you're on stage, so I played the entire scene with my back away from the audience. As I came running off, I quickly whispered to the dresser that I thought it had torn.

But the next costume fit the same way. And so did the one after that. And the one after that. I couldn't figure out what had happened.

By intermission I was in a panic.

I kept asking the dresser, "What's with all my costumes? Something's the matter with them."

She just looked the other way and wouldn't answer.

I checked through the rack and found they had all

been altered. I could see where the seams had been let out. No wonder they were three sizes too big.

I went running to the stage manager.

"Hey, what's going on? My costumes have been altered!"

He snarled back at me, "No, they haven't! Come on! You're going to be late! Get out there!"

I was utterly confused. Were they trying to gaslight me? I knew they didn't like me much. Was this some kind of vicious farewell present? But I did what he told me and played the rest of the show looking and feeling like a fool. It was excruciating.

When the curtain finally came down, I ran straight to wardrobe and confronted the wardrobe mistress.

"Did you alter my costumes?"

She looked at me as if she couldn't comprehend what I was so excited about.

"Well, yes, I did. We're going on the road. I had to get them ready for Joanna Pettet. It was all authorized."

I freaked.

"But I have three more performances to play! You altered the costumes for Joanna Pettet? Fine! Let Joanna Pettet play it! I'm not showing up at this theater until those costumes have been altered back!"

An audience had gathered outside the wardrobe-room door. It was a better show than what we had been doing on stage.

The stage manager pushed his way through and interposed himself protectively in front of the wardrobe mistress.

"If you mean what you say and don't do the show, Miss Ashley, we'll have to take you up on Equity charges."

"Go ahead!" I screamed. "Take me up on Equity charges! Nobody's going to treat me like that!"

The next morning I stormed into the producer's office

in a blind rage and sputtered out what had happened. He had already heard about it. He was not impressed. I couldn't seem to get across how humiliated and betrayed I felt.

"How could more consideration be given to a lazy wardrobe mistress than to an actress who has to go out there and do a show every night? How could they let me go on stage without telling me? How could they lie about it afterwards?"

He dismissed my tirade with a smile. It was just Bessie Von Bitch off on another meaningless, childish rampage.

"Oh, all right, Elizabeth. If it's going to get you so upset, we'll have them altered back by this evening. Okay? Case closed. I don't think there's anything more to say about it."

I called him every name in the book and ran off in tears.

I suppose it had pushed all my neurotic buttons at once.

The whole thing made me feel like I did when I was a child back in school and they told me, "You don't count. You don't matter. You're just a piece of meat."

Something in me still believed that was true. But there was another part of my spirit that could no longer accept it.

Oh, no, I'm not!

I am *not* a piece of meat!

I *do* matter!

I *do* count!

I *am* somebody!

I am!

I am!

Baton Rouge, 1949

12

"Attention, class! Pencils on your desks! Legs together! Eyes straight ahead! I will now pass out the tests. Do *not* turn them over until I give the signal to begin!"

Miss Glen barked out the instructions like the WAC sergeant she had been until she returned to Baton Rouge the year before and began teaching fourth grade at Dufroque Elementary. As always, we snapped to and followed her orders to the letter.

She moved briskly across the front row, stopping in front of each child just long enough to slap down a test paper and satisfy herself no crib notes were hidden away.

I was terrified. Miss Glen aways scared me, and I was sure I was going to flunk. I must have read that chapter on Malaya a dozen times, but the facts just wouldn't stick in my head. I never was able to learn anything I couldn't personalize, and none of the stuff about banyan trees, rain belts, and Dyaks made any sense at all.

When I had told my mother how lost I felt in geography, she said, "Well, you jus' sit there with that book and study. You sit there and do it, that's all."

I realized it was humiliating for her that I was such a poor student, so I did what she told me. I tried my best, but I knew it wouldn't be good enough.

The closer Miss Glen came to my seat in the back row, the more frightened I became. When she glanced over in my direction, I sat up extra straight. There was a slight smile on her face. It wasn't for me. It had to be for Marjorie Merrick, the girl who sat in front of me.

Everybody loved Marjorie Merrick, even Miss Glen. She had all the A-list boyfriends and girlfriends. She was in the A-list scout troop. She was an A-list student. Marjorie Merrick had it all. If my fairy godmother appeared and asked me who I wanted to be, I would have answered, "Marjorie Merrick!" without a second's hesitation.

Marjorie smiled back at Miss Glen, then reached down and picked up her geography book and cracked it open for a last look. Miss Glen hadn't gotten back to us yet, so we were allowed to do that.

I suppose that because I wanted to be like Marjorie Merrick I picked up my book and looked at it too, and then I bent down to put it away. When I straightened back up, the test was sitting on my desk.

"Ready, class. You may now . . . *begin!*"

I quickly read down the first four questions. To my astonishment, I knew the answers to three of them.

Which island in the East Indies has the largest population?

It was Java!

What are Sumatra's most valuable exports?

Coffee and sugar!

Name three large animals found in Borneo.

Wild oxen, orangutans, and wild pigs!

I congratulated myself and started to write them in when my test paper suddenly vanished. I looked up, and there was Miss Glen crumpling it in her hand. She glared down at me and hissed, "See me after school!"

I couldn't understand what was happening. What had I done wrong? Before I was able to get the question out of my mouth, she was back on guard in the front of the room.

I sat there at attention, with the fear gnawing away

at my stomach, listening to everyone else scribble down their answers. After the bell rang and they all filed out into the freedom of Friday afternoon, I was still sitting there. I could hear them whooping and laughing on the other side of the window as Miss Glen began to mark the papers. She never looked up once. There was no acknowledgment that I was still there.

I didn't know what I was supposed to do, but after the sounds of the other children playing had long faded, I cautiously walked up to her desk.

"Miss Glen, what have I . . . ? Why did you take my . . . ? What did I do?"

Her face was filled with loathing.

"You know what you did!"

"I don't know. Please, what did I do?"

"You were cheating! Do you think I didn't see you pull out your book?"

"But Miss Glen. Marjorie Merrick was sitting there and I saw M—"

"Are you trying to tell me Majorie Merrick was cheating?"

"No. She wasn't. But I saw her pull out her book, so I thought it was all right to have a last look."

"Don't lie to me! Don't ever lie to me again! Now get yourself out of here!"

I ran from the room in tears. Nothing like that had ever happened before, and it scared and hurt me. I still didn't know what it was, but I felt as if I *had* done something wrong, that there *was* something wrong with me.

I had always felt there was something wrong with me and that I was asking too much of the world. I suppose I was asking the world to assure me I was okay. And now that Miss Glen said I wasn't, it was like my last court of appeals.

I had to get home and tell my mother. She always

said I could tell her anything. That was our secret pact. My mother knew it was hard for me staying with Crazy Nanny, my grandmother, while she was working. But she couldn't do anything about it. She was trapped. We were all trapped with each other.

I hurled myself across Government Street without even looking at the light. There was a sudden squeal of tires, and I froze in my tracks. The driver of the maroon Dodge stuck his head out of the window and hollered at me.

"You *stupid* kid! What the hell's the *matter* with you?"

Nanny was waiting on the front porch.

"*Elizabeth!* Where have you been? Don't you know what time it is? You bad child! What kind of mischief were you up to?"

I pretended not to hear and ran into the house. Granddaddy was sitting at the kitchen table listening to his radio show as he sneaked a hit off of his Four Roses.

"I want to talk to my Mama!" I sobbed at him.

He started to tell me something when the screen door slammed closed again. Nanny was still in pursuit.

"Don't you dare bother your mother when she gets home!" she yelled. "She's got enough on her mind without worryin' about you!"

I clenched my lips closed and glared at her with hatred. She went into her heart attack routine.

"Oh, my heart, my heart! Where's my medicine? That child is goin' to be the death of me!"

I slipped past her and ran into the living room. When she finally quieted down, I sat in the chair by the window and searched out the street for my mother, keeping myself coiled to dash out from the house if she took it in her head to come after me and give me a whipping.

It was always like that between us. I was Nanny's adversary and she was mine. We were enjoined in battle from the moment of my birth, because the one real act of defiance my mother had committed was marrying my father. "That man is trash, Lucille, white trash!" she had screamed when my mother came home with the engagement ring. "You go off with him and you'll never set foot in this house again!" And sure enough, when my mother left him shortly after I was born, she had to beg Nanny to let her back in. Nanny never let her forget it, not even when my mother ended up having to support her and my grandfather on a clerk-typist's salary.

I was a living reminder of my mother's defiance. Nanny loved to tell her that because she was divorced and had a child, she was like the woman who wore the scarlet letter and had to be very, very careful or people would think we were trash. Then she would look at me because she knew who the little piece of trash was. It was sitting right there in that room.

Finally my mother came walking down the street. She looked even more exhausted and depressed than she usually did. Sometimes she would break down and cry as soon as she came in the door. She was always terrified of being fired. That job was our lifeline, and if she lost it we would starve.

I jumped up and ran out to meet her. On the way back inside I tried to tell her what had happened, but she was so tired and drained she couldn't understand it.

"Are you sure you weren't cheatin'? If you were cheatin' . . ."

"No, Mama, I wasn't. I wasn't!"

"Well, you weren't makin' good grades. Are you sure? You don't have to lie about it."

I did lie a lot as a kid. I got told the story of the "Little Boy Who Cried Wolf" so often I knew every detail by heart. But I wasn't lying then. Yet I couldn't get her to believe me.

She just shook her head and said, "Oh my God, I jus' don't know what I'm goin' to do with you, child."

I looked out the window, and there was my Aunt Cissy crossing the block. She was a nurse in New Orleans and sometimes came to visit us, but we weren't expecting her then.

"Look, Mama! There's Aunt Cissy!"

She threw up her hands in despair.

"My God, Elizabeth! You've got to stop that. Cissy's not comin'. I know you jus' want to change the subject and not talk about it any more."

I said, "No, really. There's Cissy. Look!"

She raised herself from her chair and grudgingly peered out the window. When she saw Cissy walking up the driveway she whispered, "All right, Elizabeth, don't tell anyone about this. Jus' keep it to yourself. Go back to school Monday, do the best you can, and try to make up your grade on the next test. Now run outside and play till supper's ready."

I gave Cissy a quick kiss hello, and sprinted out the door. I knew where I had to go. The garage. It was the one place I could truly be myself, the one place I was sure to be all right.

Neither my mother nor the neighbors who lived in the other half of the house had a car, so the garage was used as a storeroom for discarded junk nobody wanted but couldn't quite bear to throw away. It was just a dumping ground for worn-out lawn furniture, boxes of old clothes, five-year-old magazines, bulb catalogues, and broken curtain rods and fishing poles. But to me it was a refuge and a sanctuary. I could make it into anything I

246

wanted. A palace. A garden. An enchanted island. A robber's den. Anything.

I felt better as soon as I closed the door behind me and took the first hot, musty breath. This was more like it. Now to get to it.

I picked up an old *Collier's* magazine and flipped through the pages, looking for the mysterious, tormented, windswept women who illustrated the stories, No, not today. I tossed the magazine aside and continued to putter about.

Perhaps I would do my ballerina. That was always one of my favorites. Yes, I was a great ballerina, but I had a weak heart and if I ever danced again I would die.

I cleared a space in the center of the room and went to the empty orange crate where I had hidden away my toe shoes and tutu from dancing school. There wasn't much time. I changed my clothes quickly and began.

The Count tapped on my dressing room door.

I recognized the sound of his cane.

"Come in, Pierre," I called.

He wore evening clothes and carried a bouquet of long-stemmed yellow roses.

"For you, my precious. A simple token of my love and admiration."

"Oh, Pierre, thank you. They are so beautful."

"Not half as beautiful as you are. Will you dance for me tonight?"

I dared not. It would mean my death. But he loved me so, how could I refuse him?

"Only for you, my love. Only for you will I dance."

They raised the curtain and I glided out onto the stage. The audience was waiting for me, hoping I would go on. They stood up from their seats and cheered. I bowed respectfully and nodded to the conductor. The orchestra began playing the *Mirror Variations* from *Faust*.

I never danced better in my life. The audience was transfixed by my brilliance. Pierre smiled from the wings and threw me kisses.

I felt myself gasp. Yes, my heart was going. But somehow I had to make it through to the end. Summoning up all my failing strength, I willed myself into the final turns. The theater exploded with applause. Pierre was moved so deeply he smiled and cried at the same time.

I took a deep, deep bow and steadied myself with my fingertips to keep from passing out. The ushers carried baskets of flowers to the stage. The audience gave me a standing ovation. Pierre reached into his cape and pulled out a pearl necklace. Everything was getting dim. They lowered the curtain just in time.

"I told her what would happen if she danced again."

The doctor took off his stethoscope and shook his head sadly.

"What a pity. Such a great artist and to die so young."

Pierre knelt down and clasped my hand. The tears ran down his face.

"What have I done, my darling? Can you forgive me? I didn't know. I didn't know."

"Yes, I forgive you," I whispered.

I could just make out the people standing behind him. There was the conductor, my dancing teacher, Marjorie Merrick, Miss Glen, my mother, Crazy Nanny.

I opened my arms and called out to them with my final breath.

"I forgive you too. I forgive you all."

I closed my eyes for the very last time.

"*Elizabeth!* What in the world is goin' on? What are you *doin'* down there?"

248

My eyes opened with a start. Nanny was hovering above me.

"Supper's been on the table for half an hour. My God, child, why are you wearin' your dancin' clothes?"

I didn't know what to say. How could I explain it to her? I just lay there staring up at her and mumbled that I would be along directly. She threw up her arms in exasperation and shuffled back to the house.

I waited until the screen door slammed closed, then got up and changed back into my jeans. They were all talking in the living room while I ate in the kitchen. When I was through washing my dishes I excused myself to tell them good night. I was tired and wanted to go to bed.

Lying there in the dark I thought about tomorrow. It was Saturday. I only had dancing class in the morning. I could go back to the garage in the afternoon.

Maybe I would do Nancy Drew and solve the murder with my boyfriend. I could clear my father's name and he would no longer be a fugitive hunted by the law.

Perhaps I'd be the little rich girl who was kidnaped. The kidnapers would tie me up and stick a gag in my mouth, but I'd have my mother's paring knife taped to my wrist and when they came to do away with me, boy, would they be surprised. I would overcome them all and be a heroine. My picture would be on the front page and everyone would interview me and ask for my autograph.

Or I might make myself a prom queen like Jane Powell in *A Date With Judy* and sing "It's a Most Unusual Day."

All of that could come true in the garage.

In the garage I *was* prom queen.

In the garage I *was* a great ballerina.

In the garage I *was* glamorous and wicked and an adventuress and a seductress.

I could be anyone I wanted in the garage. I could be

an outlaw. A movie star. Cleopatra, the Queen of the Nile.

In the garage I never lost.

In the garage I always won.

So what else could I have grown up to be?

When someone asks me, "When did you know you wanted to be an actress?" I cannot really answer the question. I only know that looking back over my life with a moderate degree of intelligence, what else could I have been? Where else could I have gone? It was in the dice.

All I have ever wanted was to get back to the garage. It was the only place where I ever won. The only place where there was no one to say, "You cheat and you lie. You're damaged goods. You don't count. You are a burden. You should never have been born."

I had to become an actress. I didn't have any choice. It was the only thing I could do, the only thing that made me feel credible and worthwhile. After all the years of self-destruction and failure and not being good enough, it was the one thing that stood between me and being a washed-out, third-rate human being.

All the things that are negative in me as a person—the incompetence and despair and weakness and pain—are like a gift from God in a performer. If you don't hide them and if you stop lying to yourself about what you are and are not, there is a ring or a tent or a stage where you can take them and use them to make something beautiful. Because drama is made up of what people most fear and deny in themselves. The taboos. The secrets. The devils and the demons. The only reason they let us live, I suppose, is because somebody has to confront what those things are like and tell other people about them.

I could give a fine, maybe even great performance in *Cat on a Hot Tin Roof* because I know the pain and the failure and the third-rateness that Maggie feels. But the play is different from my life because in the play Maggie is triumphant. She wins by giving salvation to another person, and the only salvation I have to give is on that stage. Maybe that's why I work all the time. Whenever I'm not working, when I leave the garage and go back to the house, my sense of inadequacy begins to take over again.

I am an undereducated, rather weak human being who lucked into the one place on the planet where people like me are necessary. Through the grace of God I found a stage and was able to hang on long enough to where they let me get up on it, and that's the only reason for someone like me to be alive. I have to try to be an artist because if I give that up I will blow it everywhere else.

But it's okay to be a cripple if there's a place where you can dance. I think that's fair. I've never argued with that one. And I think that's what performers are. We are the cripples whom God has blessed. He said to us, "You, you get to dance," and that's the balance. But I have to remember that I can dance only because I am a cripple. Sometimes I get so heady and so confident when I get out on the stage that I do forget it, and that's when my legs buckle under me and I start to break.

The stage is the only place where I have ever been aware of getting approval and acceptance and love and appreciation and respect and trust, so it's perfectly evident to me that that's where I'm supposed to be. I think my life has really just been a search for my turf, for my place. There has to be a place for everyone, and I've found mine. I'm able to be a good person on the stage. I'm able to do it right. And when I'm not good, it's not because I've cheated and lied and it's not because I didn't try.

I feel strong and brave on the stage, and I don't feel especially strong or brave anywhere else. The only strength and courage I have when I'm not on the stage are the excess left over from having been there. If the day ever comes when they won't let me go out there any more, I don't know what will happen to me. They'll have to kill me. They'll have to club me to death. But then as a performer you never know. It could be tomorrow that everything changes and you may never get a good job again. You may never get any job again. When you're hot you're hot. When you're not you're not. That's the way it goes.

But as long as I can continue to get back to that protected space, that sacred ground, I know I'll always be able to start clean. It doesn't matter what happened before or what happens when it's over. You stand or fall on who you are at that moment in time and space and the universe.

Then.

There.

That place.

That night.

That minute.

There's nothing before.

There's nothing after.

You do it or you don't do it.

It is simple.

It is clear.

It is absolute.

It is the only absolute I know.

Strengths

1 attractive
2 can handle people effectively
3 love church + participation in it
4 strong will + endurance
5 the belief that I can handle anything I set out t~~

Weaknesses

1 giving with grace - Impatient - fixing
that are messed up. Wanting you to have a good
2 ill tempered. Not wanting to like my mother
3 falling for wrong man + forgetting all plan
of marrying a man thats to my advantag

Possibilities

1 training in real estate

2 education

3 holding a job

4 creative go getter
selling crafts

5 Striving to sell

6 Learning to love & appreciate peop

7 personality course

8 cast aside ~~useless~~ mental baggage - Work on Effec